The Divine
Ultimate Transformer

A Philosophy for Living
With Messages for a Lifetime

Isiah Paul "The Prophet" Ward, J.D.

The author is available for book signings and lectures. For information, contact the publisher.

Published by Millennium Bridge, Inc.
303 Waterford Dr., Willowbrook, IL 60527 – 5463

Editing: Dr. Martha Ward Plowden

Graphic Designer and Inside Layout: Nelson Grant

Printed in the United States of America

Library of Congress Control Number: 2009911133

ISBN: 978-0-9749792-4-3

Dedication

To those desiring to grow, unfold and attain cosmic consciousness.

Acknowledgements

Thanks to all my lovely family members and dear friends for transmitting positive vibration, wonderful thoughts, their never ending love and allowing me to do what I was sent here to do. The following set forth my inspiration to write this book:

"Now go, write it before them in a table and note it in a book, that it may be for the time to come for ever and ever."

Isaiah 30: 8

"Also I heard the voice of the Lord saying, Whom shall I send, and who will go for us? Then said I, Here am I; send me."

Isaiah 6:8

Introduction

I was divinely inspired and greatly motivated to write this book. The content of this book is not like what you are accustomed to reading. However, you do not have to be an erudite to understand it, but you need to read it with an open mind and heart to gain a greater understanding. My empirical research concerning worldly events indicates that humankind is retrogressing in their mental, physical and spiritual actions to a primitive barbarian state of living. Until we understand homicides are suicides, we will continue to kill ourselves through personal conflict and warring with others. We must learn to love and respect one another like ourselves and subscribe to the saying, *"Treat others as you want them to treat you."* If we were to live by the one universal principle of love, we would have a world without crime, fear, hate, envy, jealous or greed. It is of paramount importance that we practice daily loving one another and saying only that which would make us love. Further, we must learn that the only person who can really stop insulting or hurting him/herself or another person is the person inflicting the hurt. It is interested to note that most all religions subscribe to the universal principle of "The Golden Rule," even though their words may not be the same, but the meaning remains the same. The Biblical Scripture in *The Living Bible*, Matthew 7:12 states, "Do for others what you want them to do for you." It is imperative that we reverse our thinking from greed and fear to a loving peaceful giving world, if not we could be on a path of self-destruction. When we learn to change our thinking and practice to the true meaning of love and free giving, then unquestionably, we will live in a different kind of world filled with love, peace, joy and happiness. Then we can proudly say, "I will send forth my actions and words into the world so that all mankind may see and hear; therefore all my actions and words must be good and true."

We must become aware of our wrong doings and get in touch with our inner selves. Further, we must stop constantly seeking that which our bodies need and if we do not get it; we will take it by might of physical strength rather than doing what is right. It is important that we elevate our thinking and living from a primitive barbarian way in that, we must take what we want by the power of might-over-right. Such practice is still a part of our present day standard of civilization, whereas we kill and exploit others for mere personal gain. Is this the civilized way? *I think not.* We must reach the stage in our unfolding where we must learn the facts of universal law and practice them faithfully because; *"If you live by the sword, you will die by the sword."* That old way of life, which foster hate and fear, must be abandoned.

This book will serve, as a guide for individuals to unfold in the direction of his/her ultimate goal toward attaining cosmic consciousness/awareness. Dr. Richard M. Bucke coined the phase cosmic consciousness; his premise is that during the course of humanity's evolutionary development there are three forms of consciousness:

1. Simple Consciousness, our instinctual consciousness.
2. Self-consciousness, that self-awareness that allows a human to realize himself as a distinct entity.
3. Cosmic consciousness, a new developing faculty at the pinnacle of our evolution.

Cosmic awareness is an experience that comes suddenly without warning with a sensation of being immersed in a flame or rose-colored

cloud. It is accompanied by a feeling of ecstasy, moral and intellectual illumination in which, like a flash, a clear conception in outline is
presented to the mind of the meaning and drift of the universe. The
person having this experience knows that the universe is a living presence that life is eternal, the soul of man is immortal, the foundation
principle of life is love, and the happiness of every individual in the
long run is certain. All fear of death, all sense of sin is lost and the
personality gain added charm and is transformed. In a few moments
of the experience, the individual will learn more rather than in years or
month of study in institutions, schools or universities further, they will
learn and know that no study can compare to this experience.

Down through the ages, we have had prophets, messengers,
sages, deep thinkers and others who have given us information for
righteous living spiritually, mentally, physically and emotionally. The
question remains, have we heeded their calls? I think not, at least not
to the extent that we have become an enlighten people. By not adhering, we are surely paying for it in our life experiences. Dr. Bucke
names thirteen individuals who attained cosmic consciousness, and to
whom we should increasingly strive to emulate. They are: Gautama,
Jesus, Paul, Platinus, Mohammed, Dante, Las Casas, John Ypes, Francis Bacon, Jacob Behmen, William Blake, Balzac and Walt Whitman.
These individuals tried to give us a message of love so we would be
enlighten to care and treat our neighbors like ourselves.

My inspiration for writing this book is to put forth and expand
on some core philosophical principles for living a righteous loving
life, as previously done by others. I feel this book will serve as a
blueprint for living and maintaining a joyous, happy, loving, peaceful,
beautiful life experience. This information about these all-important
subjects, *Self, Life, Relationship and Death*, are yet to be exhausted;
however, I am compelled to start the dialogue here in this book. The
messages in each chapter is thought provoking, motivational and helpful for us to raise our consciousness/awareness level, so we may trans-

form ourselves to the highest level in this life experience. We must rededicate ourselves to be the best person humankind has to offer. In addition, we must learn to meet force with gentleness, impatience with patience, hate with love, fear with joy, greed with giving, misunderstanding with understanding and negativism with positivism. This book has four chapters with subchapters, the first chapter is about *Self*; which discusses knowing who you are, what you can and should become and how you can achieve your goals and have a peaceful happy life. The second chapter is about *Life*; it has subchapters on *Healthy Living, Religion, Employment and Retirement.* The third chapter is about *Relationship,* in this chapter I introduce the word my lovely wife coined, "Welationship" (meaning: togetherness and connectedness). The subchapters are about: *Marriage, Opposite Sex Friendship, Parenting and Toxic Family Members.* The fourth chapter is titled *Death;* this chapter deals with understanding that death is not final, but a beginning; also there are suggestions on pre-death planning in order to make it easier on the deceased survivors. The information contained in these chapters and subchapters is a philosophy for one to live out his or her life experiences.

It is my wish, hope and prayer that this truth will guide us from a barbaric way of thinking and lead us to rejoicing and living in a state of ecstasy. Be mindful this book is not exhaustive on these topics I choice to write about, but it is a great beginning. It is up to others to conduct further in-depth research and report their findings to promote peace, justice and the good for all humankind. Furthermore, as you progress throughout your life experience, it is my desire that you conduct your own personal research for the purpose of seeking out your own truth. It is imperative for you to know, believe, except and remember that there is no truth until you decide your won truth. It is an incontrovertible fact that truth cannot be restricted, it has no boundaries and it cannot be buried.

In all probability, you will find this book unlike any other you might have read. So, I strongly suggest after you have completed reading this book that you reread it over and over very slowly, prayerfully and meditatively in order to fully digest its content. After each chapter, I will include some of my new "*Wardisms*" that I am famous for creating.

(This word is licensed under the Creative Commons, this license allows for redistribution, commercial and non-commercial, as long as it is passed along unchanged and in whole, with credit to the author).

Edwin Markham said: *"In vain do we build the city if we do not first build the man."*

GET READY TO TRANSFORM YOUR WAY OF THINKING!

*TURN THE PAGE, YOUR
TRANSFORMATION BEGINS NOW.*

Contents

1
SELF

Know Thyself

It has been reported the phrase, *"Know Thyself"* was inscribed over a gateway of the Temple of Apollo. Further, credit was given to the Greek philosopher Socrates as the one who popularized the phrase. To *"Know Thyself"* is to have a greater insight into our minds and know who we are, if we do not like who we are, we can change and become better individuals. Also, knowing thyself will help us to overcome our illnesses physically, mentally spiritually and emotionally. To *"Know Thyself"* is a fundamental tenet of the question of life's meaning. To truly know oneself involves a deeply personal spiritual transformation whereby one seeks to orient him/herself toward understanding his/her own reality, in order to gain earnest insight into aspects of one's own life experience. Knowledge of oneself is the only real knowledge of understanding and knowing thyself; only then may one truly under-stand another. This ancient truism of *"Know Thyself"* was taught by enlightened sages and wise men of old.

For a person to know him/herself is to know and feel that there is no human master, for nature is his/her servant. When human fails to grasp their authority they sink to the level of the lowest animal. Anyone can command your actions and dictate your thoughts; if you are told to "go" you will not hesitate to go. If you are instructed to come, you will come willingly. This is the way animals respond by performing the will of their masters. There is no master to favor but the Almighty Divine Supreme Creator. No one should live on the achievement of others, by doing so you admit their superiority at the risk of your inferiority. When you know yourself, you firmly know that you are the leader in charge of your own life journey and accept it as a marathon and not a sprint. Always refuse the right of any man's superiority over you, fear no man every man is your equal. Always maintain composure of yourself by being calm and in control of your thoughts. Also, always choose your thoughts wisely before speaking and then you will not make a fool of yourself. When you make a fool of yourself you lose your human faculties to reason, which cause you to lose your mental balance. Furthermore, it is important to be self-sufficient, never depend on another person to support you. That is why it is important to choose your employment or an occupation that would give you the greatest satisfaction and then you will put your whole heart and soul into it and achieve your greatest good.

Once you know yourself, you will have supreme love and re-spect for yourself, as well as humankind. Then you will know the answer to: **Who you think you are may not be who you truly are.** When you truly know yourself, you have a greater appreciation and a tremendous respect for humankind. This will help you live a peace-ful happier life and remain in a state of ecstasy. Men and women's supreme desire is to love and equally be loved. However, they create fear and hate and then allow that fear and hate to destroy them until they realize that love is ultimately the way. All created things have sufficient knowledge or instinct for their individual survival. There is a familiar phrase, "As we think, so we become," moreover, it should be added, "As we do, so we become," because we are a result of our decisions we put into action. By knowing yourself, you will always strive toward building a better life for your family and yourself, as well as help others to fulfill their desires, which should be your ulti-mate reason for living. The body will perform as the mind instructs it, when it is ill, it is out of balance. You can only restore your mind to complete balance by thinking righteous thoughts.

When you truly know yourself, you will trust your own counsel and ask or receive no advice from anyone. Not everybody has your best interest at heart, no one can advise you unless he/she becomes immerse as a part of you. They must see your problem as their problem and your desire for its solution must be their desire too. No one can know your entire problem, nor can you sufficiently explain it to him or her. More often then not, they cannot fully grasp it and more importantly they are not willing to assist you; the exception would be a professionally trained counselor. The other exception is when both spouses are in tuned with each other, well connected, working together, thinking together for the greater good of their relationship and working together with the Almighty Divine Supreme Creator as one. You must know and remember, the answer to your every question lies within yourself, because complete knowledge (omniscience) centers our consciousness. Therefore, before you ask anyone to answer a question for you; it will be of great benefit if you first meditate upon it and desire to know the answer from within yourself. You will grow mentally and spiritually stronger, feel better about yourself, and find yourself being a very different kind of person. Then you will find yourself increasingly dependent upon no one but yourself, as well as being certain of yourself. Further, it will help you to conquer any self-defeating behavior and/or attitude you may have about yourself.

When you find yourself faced with a problem, it is important to know how to positively deal with it. First, search within your conscious to find how or where you have violated the law of balance. Do not seek the answer outside of yourself or tell anyone your problem that is not willing to take on your problem as their own, with the exception of the individuals previously mentioned. Conversely, if you decide to take on someone else problem make certain it is your decision not theirs. Once again, seek your answer from within. Even though someone with knowledge about your problem can open the door to it for you, but you must enter through the door yourself. Another person may inspire you to gain knowledge for yourself, as well as awaken the power that lies dormant within you. Know that it is extremely important to take breaks and periodically silent yourself, in order to balance your thinking. There is an old proverb that said, "Sometimes it is best to be silent and thought of as a fool than to speak and remove all doubts." Also, Nicolaus Copernicus, a Polish astronomer said: "To know that we know what we know, and to know that we do not know, that is true knowledge."

It is extremely important to seek and find your originality and create things that will benefit humankind. Then you can hold your head high and know you are the ruler of yourself. You will know that you rule yourself through your mind by always thinking highly and deeply of and about yourself. Know that you are created divinely, if you do not, you will treat yourself and allow others to treat you any old way. In addition, know that knowledge is everywhere, some of it is hidden, so search for it and you will discover it; then you are able to share it with humankind to make a better world to live in. Always keep your body, mind and soul in tune and in balance with the laws of the universe so you will not ever lose your sense of perception. Try and always maintain a strong will and emphasize your will by having factual information to support your beliefs. Your will is your decision, and your decision is your intelligence, and your intelligence is your personality, and your personality is your self-confidence and your true being. It is important to always have a purpose in life and that purpose must be well thought out and be a true representation of who you are, as well as how you want to be portrayed. Always cherish your time, wasting time is non-essential, there is nothing to be achieved by wasting time, it can never be recalled or regained. Someone said, "If you kill time, you murder success." Let your efforts be toward finding something tangible to do and make major contributions to the betterment of humankind. Always act and present yourself as a divine created being, as you are, and never allow anyone to convince you to see or think that you are inferior. Allow yourself to rise in dignity to justify all that is noble and good about your life experiences. You must always seek the right way and be righteous in your giving and receiving, never, never ever hang around people who are always discouraging, despondent, mentally poverty-stricken, poor thinkers and never want to do well for themselves and/or humankind. If so you will ultimately become like them. When you associate with happy and prosperous people, you will unconsciously take on their happiness and prosperity way of life, this power was given to you as your birthright. In *The Greatest Miracle In the World*, written by Og Mandino, he talked about how the Almighty Divine Supreme Creator endowed humankind with unlimited powers unknown to any other creature in the universe, such as:

- I gave you the power to think.
- I gave you the power to love.
- I gave you the power to will.
- I gave you the power to laugh.
- I gave you the power to imagine.
- I gave you the power to create.
- I gave you the power to plan.
- I gave you the power to speak.
- I gave you the power to pray.

Og Mandino added that the Almighty Divine Supreme Creator had such pride in the creation of humankind that no limits were spared. We are the ultimate creation, the greatest miracle, a complete divine living being. We are able to adapt to any climate, any hardship and/or any challenge. We are capable of putting our own destiny in motion. Also, we have the awesome ability to translate a sensation or perception by our thoughts and to make them into whatever action is best for all humanity and thyself. In addition, the Creator gave us the ultimate ability and the power to choose right over wrong, good

over bad, happiness over sadness, love over hate, laughter over crying, creating over destroying, persevering over quitting, praising over
gossiping, healing over wounding, giving over stealing, praying over
complaining, growth over stagnation and to live rather than just exist.
We are capable of these and many other great wonders and should
never limit ourselves while living out our life experiences. The map
of life has been given to us, so all we have to do is to chart our destiny
and navigate successfully, even though there may be some rough and
challenging times ahead.

Knowledge lies within all of us because our Almighty Divine
Supreme Creator is within each of us; you are then the Creator in
the measure of your awareness. The Biblical Scripture in *The Living
Bible*, Luke 17: 20-21 says:

> One day the Pharisees asked Jesus, "When will the King-
> dom of God begin? Jesus replied, The Kingdom of God
> isn't ushered in with visible signs. You want be able to say,
> 'It has begun here in this place or there in part of the coun-
> try.' For the Kingdom of God is within you."

To this extent, you must know your inner vision can see what your
outer vision cannot see, as well as your inner ears can hear what your
outer ears cannot hear. The terms "inner vision" and "inner ears" really means no more than mind awareness. When you are inspired
to know this, then you have become aware of your divinity. This is
what the sages and divine teachers of the past were trying to teach
us. Their words were filled with very plain admonitions to tell us that
mortal persons could not have knowledge or power of their own, until
they are able to see and know the Almighty Divine Supreme Creator.
Those who come to know the Almighty Divine Supreme Creator in-
timately moment-to-moment see much with their inner vision that is
otherwise forever hidden to those who just sense and never know.
The ultimate of such a transformation is cosmic consciousness, which
means your mind becomes in oneness with the Almighty Divine Su-

preme Creator's mind. Sadly, as mortal beings, we gradually or rarely become aware of our immortality. The Biblical Scripture in *The Living Bible*, John 14: 10-11, Jesus said:

> Don't you believe that I am in the Father and the Father is in me? The words I say are not my own but are from my Father who lives in me. And he does his work through me. Just believe it – that I am in the Father and the Father is in me. Or else believe it because of the mighty miracles you have seen me do.

Once you realize you are one with the Almighty Divine Supreme Creator, and then you will accept the basis of your omniscience (having total knowledge), your omnipotence (having unlimited power) and your omnipresence (being present everywhere). These omni attributes are within you, only you can awaken them from their dormant state from within you. By sufficiently meditating on your problem/issue and allowing the answer to first come from within yourself, then you should know what is best for yourself. Once again, be cautious of advice from others, only accept it to the extent that you have information, reason and judgment to fully understand its value, otherwise it may be harmful. Do not rely on a genius, a prophet or anyone to interpret your life for you. You must tap into your own genius from within, allow that prophetic voice from within direct, and guide you through your destiny. Everyone inherited his or her genius within at birth, it is not limited to some people but all people, omniscience is universal. You can view it from the standpoint that all humankind are created equal by virtue of the divinity of their creation, therefore all human rights are intrinsic to human creation and thus inalienable. Further, each person can know all things when they desire to know all things. Always maintain a strong will in order to derive at a conclusion that you know is right for you. In order to come to that conclusion, you must have the facts before you. Your facts must be the best you can possibly garner on the particular matter; then do not allow anyone but

God to alter your will.

Humankind has been searching and seeking to know God since the dawn of time, Francis Trevelyan Miller, poet and historian sums it up and I quote him in part:

> Down through the centuries of human progress, we have come to the World's Greatest Adventure – Man's Search for God. And what do we find?
>
> We have found that the first and oldest fact in all human creation is man's instinct for a God – power. It has existed since the beginning of time. It took root in the intelligence of man from the day he became a human being. It has persisted through the ages as surely and as positively as his appetite for food or his instinctive grasp for breath itself...
>
> ...This search for God has covered the range of all human instincts, intuition, emotion, superstition, imagination, creative genius—every form and substance, real and unreal that the mind of man has been able to conceive...
>
> ...It has required prophets of indomitable faith and courage to blaze the way for this world-old search – the spirit of the martyrs, willing to die for an idea or a principle: Zoroaster—Moses—Guatama, the Buddhist—Mahavira and Jainism—Confucius—
>
> Lao Tze and Taoism—Jesus, the Nazarene- Mohammed...
>
> ...Today, the World is seeking more ardently than ever before the solution to this high question: <u>What is God - - and is there a life after death?</u>

The great fact of life that humankind is forever searching for their divine self and hopefully that search one day will lead them to knowing that thyself and God as one. Higher knowledge comes only to those who are lead to the light of their own divinity. Inspiration is the first steppingstone, which leads us to our higher conscious.

We will especially be inspired to know the various stages which we must pass through in the unfolding of our mental and spiritual nature before we reach the ultimate attainment, they are: mental height of Genius; then the Cosmic Conscious Illuminate and then the Christ Conscious Divine Being. In these stages, we learn to interrupt the Almighty Divine Supreme Creator's language of light, which teaches us the love nature of the Creator. The genius period is a moral period of high ideals and greater God-awareness. The genius fully comprehends the rhythms of the Creator's language and interprets those for humankind such as, music, drawing, writing, science, etc. Geniuses are the exalted ones who are quite fully aware of their divinity. They commune with the Creator for long ecstatic periods in isolation and then translate their communions into rhythmic forms to inspire others and to awaken the light in their souls. They are the ones who give the world its priceless culture. The next stage is the Cosmic Conscious period of unfolding. This is the higher moral and spiritual stage of complete God-awareness. Also, the disappearance of instinctive control, sense of evil and forgetfulness of the body distinctly mark this period. It is the stage of the mystic who is almost fully omniscient and omnipotent. The ultimate stage is Christ Consciousness, the complete awareness of unity with the Almighty Divine Supreme Creator. This is the final stage of universality, omniscience and omnipotence in humankind. Furthermore, Christ Consciousness is the connection to the Almighty Divine Supreme Creator that humans have always sensed and sought before Jesus walked the earth. Jesus came to emphasize that consciousness, not to create it. During the Christ Consciousness stage, love has been fully manifested on earth and evil has fully disappeared. According to Loa Russell in her book titled, *God Will Work With You But Not For You (1955)*, she stated:

> Jesus of Nazareth is the only man in all recorded
> history who has ever reached that stage of complete
> God-awareness. He was so fully illumined with the
> light, and the Love which God is, and the omniscience and

omnipotence which God is, that he could knowingly say: "I
and My Father are One."

The word, Christ means "The Anointed One," which was ultimately
given to Jesus; hence the names: Christ Jesus and Jesus the Christ.
Jesus was the greatest intelligentsia the world has ever known consequently he gave us the greatest teaching ever. Jesus was full and
complete in extrasensory perception. With his unlimited knowledge
and power he could do many things, which were so far beyond the
comprehension of man that they were explainable only to man as being supernatural or miraculous. The Biblical Scripture in *The Living
Bible*, John 14:12, Jesus said: "In solemn truth I tell you, anyone believing in me shall do the same miracles I have done, and even greater
ones, because I am going to be with my father."

I fell extremely compelled to further share with you my research and understanding on what is Christ Consciousness. Christ
Consciousness is the growing human recognition and blending of
the human evolutionary mind with the Divine Mind and the Divine
Personality, which is the source of human happiness and fulfillment.
This awareness accrues over time within the consciousness of human
thinking when attention and openness is focused on knowing who and
what is the "christed" state of being, which is that higher mindedness
of enlightenment. It is called "christed" state because of the sacred-
ness and purity of the individual who has achieved it. Jesus achieved
it in his human life and was given this title of "Christ" before his name
as the recognition of his achievement of this spiritual status. This path
is open to anyone regardless of their religious tradition or affiliation;
all we have to do is to be open to become a living vessel of Love
and Truth on this planet and actively strive to attain it. In the Bible,
Apostle Paul said, "Let that mind be in you which is also in Christ Jesus." This means that we all can become the incarnation of the word,
in that we can attain the level of Christ Consciousness. Just know that
there is only one power, one presence, one knower, one life, and it is

the very essence of your life. In effect, you are what you are looking for. As the cosmic anthropologists we all are, we should look not only upward to the Almighty Divine Supreme Creator as being in the sky but inward where he dwells in us. Dr. Michael A. Beckwith says in his book, *40 Day Mind Fast Soul Feast:*

> Ascend to the holy ground of your own being where
> the true Second Coming of Christ Consciousness
> takes place. We are God's manifestation on earth,
> sent here to do His will and bring forth his design.
> That is the purpose of life: to shape God's intent
> while shaping our characters and spirits, becoming
> more divine.

Some may think it is blasphemy to try and become Christ like (see above the Biblical Scripture, John 14:12); they believe that there was only one Son of God and that no one else can be like him because we are sinners. It is the concept of the original sin carried on and on generation after generation that makes people reluctant to even try to master the basic principles of life that Jesus taught. Personally, I believe it is in error to be unlike Christ. Further, I believe that it deprives Christians, Jews, Muslims and the whole world of the very essence of the life that Jesus taught and lived. In fact, it is our soul destiny to do so and not only to be aware of ourselves as the Creator, but to be aware of the Self as Father, as Son and as Holy Spirit; or as the Hindus would phrase it, "Brahma, Vishnu and Shiva." When we attain this awareness, our human minds grow and strengthen causing our lives to become more liberated, joyful, peaceful and love-domi-nated. The fear that creates isolation and despair begins to diminish in our thoughts and feelings. Then we become free to live the life we were uniquely born to live, as a child of Spirit in a love-filled and sup-portive universe. Understand, Christ is not a term used exclusively in the Christian religion, nor does it mean that you must adhere to the Christian belief system to attain this state. All of the world's religion traditions offer a path to achieving this "christed" status. However, everyone is free to find his or her own way in the context of his or her religious choice. It is important to remember that each person has his/her own path to find spiritually and to allow that path to unfold naturally for him or her. Some people find their way within the context of certain religious beliefs that the major world's religions offer; other people will find their way by blending some beliefs together in a unique and innovative way. All ways and paths are honored if they lead you into becoming more loving, forgiving, patient, kind, compassionate, tolerant, happy and at peace. All paths of Love lead to the same Source Of All That Is. Know that we all share the Creator-Source as living expressions of that Source Personality and we all are moving back home to unite with our One Source. Further, Christ Consciousness is the state of awareness of our true nature, our higher self and our birthright as children of the Almighty Divine Supreme Creator. Christ Consciousness is our living expression as a child of Spirit as we unfold our own divine life plan on this earthly plane by having heaven here on earth. Living in the full reality of our "christed" self is actually being fully alive and invested in who we truly are. Also as our "christed" self, we live as examples to inspire others to seek this path for themselves. With the hope, that one-day we can all join hands together and collectively move our planet forward into the divine plan for planetary transformation and glorification. It is the goal of all human life to evolve toward Spirit; this is the journey that unfolds over the course of our lifetime. It is the adventure of moving from time and space to eternity. Our teaching should be centered on helping people find their own internal source of Spirit. Our persona should be the embodiment of love, goodness, peace and understanding. We must allow our God-centeredness achieve what we consider miracles. When we understand the natural laws of the universe we will be able to tap into the great power of love to bring healing to people, as well as the world. We must practice meditation and prayer to gain strength to meet the challenge of daily living. I believe our purpose here on earth is two-fold: (1) Provide the living link between our Creator-Source and humanity. (2) Show each person how the Creator lives within us and to embody the Creator and reveal the Creator's love for each person who are ready to grow in Spirit. We must know, understand and accept that the Almighty Divine Supreme Creator has placed within us the resources to fulfill our journey. These resources are: the spark of cosmic consciousness, which is the flame in the heart and the three-fold flame of love, wisdom and power, which is our inner focal point of the Trinity. All we have to do is give up this mundane lifestyle and become open to being a living vessel of Truth and Love. Then we can subscribe to the saying, "Be ye in the world but not of the world." I trust and hope, I have inspired you to get in touch with and to attain the Christ Consciousness level, so you will see your Divine self that you truly are. Through Christ Consciousness you will gain a direct perception of the laws and principles that the Almighty Divine Supreme Creator used to create a sustainable universe that will not self-destruct. Therefore, by striving for Christ Consciousness, humankind will not self-destruct. Further discussion on religion and spirituality will be covered in greater detail in Chapter 3, subtitle "Religion."

It is becoming increasingly important that we need to change the way we see and interpret things. I subscribe to the belief that says, "When we change the way we look at and interpret things, the things we look at and interpret change." The Biblical Scripture in *The Living Bible*, Romans 12: 2, Paul said:

> Don't copy the behavior and customs of this world, but be a new and different person with a fresh newness in all you do and think. Then you will learn from your own experience how his ways will really satisfy you.

This does not mean the renewing of our senses or to increase the ability of our body, but to change our thought processes, in terms of how we view our life experiences. All of living is a life journey whereby we experiment in finding the right way to live our lives, so we can be and remain in a state of ecstasy. We must put forth every effort to live a good life, knowing that we become what we think. If we think negative thoughts we produce negative actions because, we choose to see things the way we want them to be for us (good or bad). James Williams said, "A great many people think they're thinking when they're merely rearing their prejudices." When we understand that negative deeds are man-made and they are not natural, we will stop allowing ourselves to think negative thoughts. We must free ourselves of negative thinking, because it is unhealthy to harbor negative thoughts about a person, place or thing. Do not continue to live in the past entertaining thoughts of bad past negative unpleasant life experiences. When you continue to think and discuss them openly, you are giving life, energy and power to them to grow and manifest. Then they are able to control and be apart of your current and future life experience. If you do not dismiss them and let them go, they will continue to haunt you throughout your life experience. When a negative thought comes to mind do not complete the thought. Stop the negative thought immediately before completing it and mentally think a dozen times, "Everything is fine, peaceful, wholesome and I am complete surrounded by God's love." We cannot just talk of brotherly love, it is equally important to act it out moment to moment in our life experience. This natural law must be obeyed, if we do not obey the law, it will not hurt the law; it hurts the violator. By way of an example, if we intentionally cut our finger with a knife, we cannot blame the injury on the knife; it is our own decision which to blame. If we were to hurt a family member or a friend and lose their friendship as a result, we alone hurt ourselves by our own decision to disobey the Creator's law of love. If we had treated them in the way we wanted to be treated by giving them love and kindness, then love and kindness will be given back to us in like measure possible overflowing. If the intrinsic essence of each religion were captured in a single short phase, the words would emphasize the importance of not harming others, such as: "Act always with loving kindness," says Buddhism. "Absence of hurtfulness is the ideal," states Hinduism. "Non-injury is the highest religion," proclaims Jainism. "Love does no wrong to a neighbor," declares Christianity. "Let a person withhold from doing harm to others," Islam declares. "Fight with no weapon but the word of God; use no means but a pure faith," asserts the scriptures of Sikhism. This is the universal law of balance, also known as, the universal law of reciprocity, which demands equality in all interchange. A seesaw is an excellent example of balance interchange. A seesaw repeatedly goes up and down when it is unequally balance, but when it is in balance both sides are equal. Also, the scales of justice are balanced when both sides are equal. This is why it is imperative that from time to time we should take breaks from the hustles and bustles of life and balance our thinking.

An individual's character speaks volume as to the kind of person he/she is and to how he/she wants to be received and respected by others. Perhaps you have never thought that you have the power and the ability to mold and shape your individual character, well you definitely do. You must refuse to be limited by other people limitations and/or expectations, let only your dreams be your boundaries. Know and accept that everyone looks different because he/she has a different body type. Each person's character and expression is different because he/she thinks and processes information differently; some adopt a feeling mode, others are auditory and even others are visual. This is the reason why it should not matter what another person says or thinks about you. However, no one has the right to ever prejudge, criticize or condemn another person regarding their actions or inactions; because you do not know what they are experiencing mentally, physically, spiritually or emotionally in their lives. On the other hand, never depend or wait to receive compliments, accolades or applauds from others to validate your existence. Surely, you have heard the saying, *"Sticks and stones may break my bones, but talk does not bother me."* From a purely philosophical point of view, it is understood that a gossiper or a slander cannot hurt you in theory; because truth is always stronger than an untruth and it rises to the forefront in the end. However, we are well aware that negative gossiping can ruin one's business, break up one's relationships and more importantly upset one's peace of mind. But never ever allow anyone to make you feel less than you are, always maintain high self-esteem. Being a little narcissist does not hurt, it could be helpful toward building one's self-esteem and self-confidence. But do not be like the prominent man walking down lover's lane holding his own hand.

This brings me back to what I wrote previously, that love alone survives and love alone is loved. We must learn that if we give love and respect to humankind, we will receive love and respect as we live out our life experiences. He/she who gives love and respect receives love and respect in like measure. Every person determines his/her own destiny by what he/she thinks and does each moment of his/her life. This is why you should never get so caught up with yesterday and let today clearly pass you by. It cannot be stated enough that one becomes what he/she wants by their righteous thoughts and actions; but the measure of their desire must be great in order for them to become great. You can reach your destiny if your desire is strong enough. However, you must be humble throughout your quest for greatness and know the quality of humility. By having the quality of humility, it gives you warm heartedness, kindness and the temperament of spiritual strength unmatched by any other. Desire alone is the controlling factor, not money, nor family members nor position in life. No one's influence can make you great; you alone control your own destiny. Many people utterly fail because they are busy blaming other conditions and/or circumstances for their failures. No one should allow alibis to be the reason for not accomplishing their destiny and blame their failure on "this and that." Every person who has ever accomplished his or her destiny did so only because of desire, planning and putting forth countless efforts. The major difference between all people lies not in their abilities, but in the difference of intensity of desire to express his/her ability. The best way to accomplish your destiny is to first visualize it mentally, then make a clear picture of it in your mind, like taking a picture of an image with a camera. This will give you a clearer picture of your destiny and help bring it into fruitions. In addition, allow your creative juices to flow freely; the creative mind must have no reservation. You cannot worry about the things you do not know about, most other people do not know about them neither. Whatever hurdles confront you, meet them with joy and full knowledge, and love the challenge to conquer them. Never say, *"I cannot do it because I do not know how to do it."* Learn how to do it by properly researching and investigating how to do it, then do it. I have people, personally, asking me about how I write my books, I humbly respond by saying, *"I get on my computer and/or take my pen and paper and start writing after I have meditated, envisioned and formulated my thoughts."* It is what I call 'free writing,' which pours out of my mind from my creative thoughts. We are always looking for the easy way out and tend to rationalize and/or justify why we cannot achieve our goals and peace of mind. I call these individuals, "human rationalists." They constantly use the following lists of excuses to explain why they can never achieve their goals or attain happiness in their life experiences (fill in the blank):

- I cannot take a chance, it to risky for me

  _____

- It will take too long for me to accomplish that

  _____

- My children and family are keeping me from

  _____

- I do not deserve receiving
  _____

- It is not my nature to do that
  _____

- I do not have enough money to afford
  _____

- I cannot get any help
  _____

- I am not smart or strong enough to do
  _____

- They change the rules when my time comes
  _____

- I am too old and do not have the energy
  _____

- My family background counts against me when
  _____

- I am afraid of doing
  _____

Do not be known as a "human rationalist," because all excuses are misplaced thoughts used to justify one's actions or inactions. Excuses make us so depressed to the point that we are sad about everything and end up doing nothing. We heard the saying, "misery loves company," some individuals' get so depressed that they plan a "Pity Party" without a meaningful purpose. They invite friends and relatives over to set around complaining and making excuses about their life's problem(s). The party attendees also set around moping and end up sharing community gossip talking about that old "he said she said mess," without accomplishing anything meaningful. It is important to realize once you rid yourselves of that inner misery and replace it with love, joy and peace, then your inner pain, suffering and misunderstanding will cease to exist. Remember, your life experience is what you create.

The basic principles in living a righteous life in all nature are truth, kindness and love. Someone once said, *"Hitch your wagon to a star and fasten its bolts with deep desire to manifest love, and behold, its wings will carry you to those heights."* Once we learn to subscribe to the universal law of love, the mundane insignificant minutia will become inconsequential. We must strive to keep balance in our social and business affairs at all times or it can be cataclysmic and fill with disorder. Also know that your physical actions will always reflect your mental thinking. Everything must be and remain in balance for nature to properly exist and function. If the earth were to stray out of its balance path ever so little, the flooding of oceans over land could immediately destroy all life. Likewise, humans can topple because of their unbalanced thoughts; our entire unfolding is the purpose of learning this lesson. In addition, when our thoughts are out of balance then our body is out of balance in the measure of our unbalanced thoughts. Equally, the universe is out of balance in the measure of our thoughts; however, we are not powerful enough to unbalance God's universe. The whole universe moves to adjust itself to our unbalance thought. We cannot have an unbalanced thought nor perform an unbalanced action without that measure of action returning to the violator in like measure. Even though the Creator gives us free will to think any thought or perform any action we desire, however the Creator holds the right to balance the unbalance by an equal reaction. In other words, our good experiences arise from our knowledge of how to produce balance thought-ideals. Conversely, our bad experiences stem from our unbalanced thought-ideals and/or action. The more knowledge we attain helps us to comply with and obey the universal laws, thereby making our lives easier and happier.

One of the greatest universal laws is the law of *BALANCE*, which enables us to tap into our genius that resides within. Geniuses know no limitation within that which is universal, as well as love and truth in all of its fullness. David R. Hawkins, M.D., Ph.D. stated in his book entitled, *Power VS Force The Hidden Determinants of Human Behavior:*

> The individual human mind is like a computer terminal connected to a giant database. The database is human consciousness itself, of which our own cognizance is merely an individual expression, but with its roots in the common consciousness of all mankind. This database is the realm of genius; because to be human is to participate in the database, everyone, by virtue of birth, has access to genius. The unlimited information contained in the database has been shown to be readily available to anyone in a few seconds, at any time and in any place.

Once we attain the genius state, we will not waste time and/or energy on anything that is not an enhancement for our spiritual growth. It is very hard for us to find complete balance alone or do good work without the loving cooperation of a balance-loving mate. A wonderful fact about the need for a balance mate is that the Almighty Divine Supreme Creator will always send us or lead us to the exact right mate at the time of our greatest need, providing we let no other motive than that of need enter into our desire. Bad mating happens when partners' motives are other than the need to have balance in their lives. All life experiences revolve around this great cosmic law, to violate it brings into focus unhappiness and sorrow. Life is too beautiful not to enjoy it fully, abundantly and rejoice in its supreme greatness.

We are God's greatest and supreme creation in all its magnificence. Humans possess the awesome ability to communicate with one another, as well as the animal kingdom. All living creatures teach their off springs the language they need to communicate with their like kind. There are multitudes of languages, sounds and symbols used to convey a thought to others. It should occur to us that everything in the universe is constantly communicating to every other thing by telling it, what it is, what it is doing and what its relationship is to other beings. We talk to nature all the time and nature is forever communicating with us. For example, an apple does not have to say, "I am an apple," its form, color, odor and taste tell us that without the need of words. However, we have identified the apple-idea by giving it a word in the human language called "apple." The nine words in nature that teach and communicate a message to all living creatures are what I call the divine nine attributes of the universal language that are: Identity, Motion, Sound, Odor, Color, Form, Temperature, Rhythm and Time.

1. *Identity*- The fact that everything is what it is and cannot be any other thing is what gives its identity. For example, in the flower family, a violet cannot be a rose nor can an oak tree be a man or vice versa; it is what it is representing its mighty creation. That is why it is critical that we identify and define who we are before someone else does.

2. *Motion*- Motion is the first step away from the static universe from which the dynamic universe is extended. All created things move in wave cycles to generate compression and heat that radiates back to the cold of its origin. Motion perpetually expresses itself to others who desire to observe its movement.

3. *Sound*- All created things emit sounds of varying kinds, however some sounds are beyond human's range of hearing. Such as fishes of the seas emit sounds that have a meaning heard by other fishes. Other animals make sounds that its like kind can hear and understand, as well as telling its identity and presence to other living beings. We emit sounds to other humans, which we call words to convey a complete thought.

4. *Odor*- Odor plays a distinctive part in relationship to the survival of human or animal. Some animals would

starve if they depended upon their eyes alone to search for food. Each odor conveys a different smell; every created being has its own distinctive odor, which spells out its identity as clearly as though it could talk and say, "I am a lemon," or "I am a rabbit," or "I am a man." How often have we gone into a room and smelled something burning in the kitchen or gas escaping from somewhere, which we could not otherwise detect? Odors are as much a part of our education as learning how to write in school. Furthermore, odors are necessary to human survival as they are for the animals in the forest.

5. _Color_- Every element or particle in the universe has its own distinctive place in the color spectrum to tell all things of its identity and purpose in creation. When we walk through a flower garden, the various colors of the flowers tell us if it is a rose, a violet, a pine or spruce tree, etc. How natural it is for all things to talk that way and have us talk to them in the same language. We must realize that we are communicating to the Almighty Divine Creator through them as directly as if we were talking to someone on a telephone, because the Almighty Divine Creator created us and everything else.

6. _Form_- Every material body has a distinctive form of its own species, which tells other forms of its identity. Each one clearly tells all other things in the universe what it is and what it can do. The form of a lemon tells its identity as clearly as its odor tells us what it is, so it is not confused with an orange. We speak through our sense of taste, as well through our sense of vision. When we look around us, every object tells us what it is and what it can do even though we might not give it a name. For example, a hammer tells us what it can do through its

existence even if we had not given it a name, etc.

7. *Temperature*- All humans, as well as other living creatures have various freezing points that tell us of their
identities in relation to other species. Temperature tells
us when water freezes or when it has reached its boiling
point, also it tells us when to put on a coat or when take it
off. Temperature alerts us when to touch or not to touch
a thing. Humans are designed by nature to withstand
a temperature normalcy of about ninety-eight degrees,
two degrees above is a warning and three more degrees
could be fatal if not alleviated quickly. On the contrary,
a human cannot live in pressure of five degrees above or
below sea level pressure. Each living thing has it own
temperature normalcy just as it has it own heartbeat and
blood pressure normalcy. These normalizations have
deep meanings and form a basis of information for us,
for our doctor and to the various scientists who specialize in animal life.

8. *Rhythm*- All effects of nature are rhythmic, which is
the heartbeat of the universe. A radical change in the
rhythm of a human heartbeat could mean death; it will
only allow a very little variation with warning or shock.
Rhythm is the basis of balance in arts, for example, in
music; the slightest variation is quite noticeable while
greater variations result in discord and out of harmony.
Rhythmic balanced interchangings are evident in all of
nature's effects from the walking of humans to the alter-
nating of piston strokes in an engine.

9. *Time*- The eternal beginning is timeless. Time is the in-
terval between sequences of events such as the pulsation
of life; there is nothing in it to count or measure. Time is
the recorder of wave frequencies and its countless varia-

tion take place in octaves manner. Time conveys countless meanings to physicist, musician, and manufacturer
and to all who lives in this civilization. Time is one
of the ways the Almighty Divine Supreme Creator processes to all living things on earth how to survive.

We must come to the realization that we all are created uniquely unto ourselves, even though we have our own idiosyncrasies; however that is what makes us unique. This is the reason we should never
allow anyone or anything to define who or what we are. The Almighty
Divine Supreme Creator gave us these divine nine attributes to lead,
guide and protect us through our existence. In addition to the divine
nine attributes, we are controlled by instinct, inspiration and imagination. Instinct is the manner in which God speaks to various forms of
living creatures. The advance form of life has reached the stage to
rely upon their senses for knowledge and/or survival through inspiration and imagination. Therefore, be extremely cautious by thoroughly researching and investigating any social, religious, business,
etc. organizations/groups before you join and commit yourself as a
devoutly devoted member. Beware, it might not be what it purports
to be. This also suggests that you must thoroughly investigate and
check the background of the organization/group leader(s); they might
be wolves in sheep clothing. Know that the leader you are looking
for stands before you in the mirror. Never be so eager to be apart of a
group just to be accepted by its members at the expense of being willing to betray your own divine given nature. Furthermore, never allow
yourself to walk in another person shadow, if you fail at something,
fail because of your doing and not because of someone else doing
or not doing what they promised to do. Even though we are in this
world, we do not have to be of this world, always be true to yourself
and do not live your life experience lusting after everything. We must
remember we are here to express that, which we must express and/or
complete in this life experience, so do not blow it. Remember who

we are change all the time, but what we are never change, so enjoy the wonder of who you are; perfect, whole and complete. When we are seen from a distance, we are judged by our appearance; however, when we walk closer to someone, they judge us by our walk and once we get even closer face to face, we are judged by our speech. Surely, you heard the saying: "An image is worth 1,000 words," no matter how illustrious you are; how brilliant you are or how attractive you are, you are still judged by how you present yourself. Research shows that it takes only four minutes for someone to make a first impression of you. In addition, according to a widely cited study conducted by UCLA professor Albert Mehrabian, body language accounts for 55% of first impression; 38% comes from your tone of voice and the remaining 7% comes from your actual words spoken. We have the responsibility to present ourselves in the best way possible in any and all situations and circumstances throughout our life experiences.

Our Almighty Divine Supreme Creator created us to be creators so that we may enjoy our human experience and live our lives fully and abundantly whereby; we can live and remain in a state of ecstasy. In order to achieve this state of ecstasy, we must learn to lose ourselves in order to find our true selves, by being in the world, but not of worldly happenings. This state of peacefulness and happiness can be attained through five-basis principles: humility, reverence, inspiration, deep purpose and joy.

1. *Humility*- No one can multiply him/herself by him/herself. We must first divide ourselves and give ourselves to the service of all humankind, by placing ourselves within all others through our acts of thoughtfulness and service. We accomplish this by suppressing our individual egos and better yet replacing them with the universal ego (being together as one). Meaning, one must not be the part, but one must be a part of the whole. The old proverbial "I" must be replaced with the all encompass-

ing "We." It is important that we must learn and accept that we are trustees of the world and ourselves.

2. _Reverence_ – It is impossible for a person to make a sale, write a book or invent anything that would improve upon humanity without first having that deep reverence. Reverence makes us know and feel that we are merely interpreters of the thought-world, who creates products to fit and enhance our life purpose. If we were to look inward toward our inner self we would be amazed at what we will find. Further, if we were alone long enough to become thoroughly acquainted with ourselves, we would hear whispering from the universal source of all consciousness that would immensely inspire us. These are actual revelations, telling us, guiding us, showing us the way to the thought-world so we are able to live our life experiences in a more peaceful harmonious way. This will enable us to find ourselves using the cosmic forces that we cannot see, instead of working blindly in the dark.

3. _Inspiration_ – Inspiration comes to us who seek it with humility and by working toward our own achievements and reverence with God. We achieve inspiration through love of our work, love of life and reverence for the universal force that gives us unlimited power for the asking. Inspiration comes to us by plugging into the universe, and then we become harmonious with its rhythms so we are able to commune with it. When we are alone, the universe talks to us in flashes of inspiration and we suddenly know things that we never knew before and we cannot explain the how or why. We do not have to learn or do anything spectacular to be inspired; it is there for the asking by recalling it and/or recognizing it as our

divine inheritance.

4. _Deep Purpose_ – There should always be a deep purpose and a well thought out plan to accomplish our goals. Absent of this we cannot bring our images and ideas into being. Once we have decided on our purpose through deep meditation, the goal to create our thought patterns and ideas into forms are easily manifested.

5. _Joy_ – We can achieve all our aims through the aspects of joy, happiness, enthusiasm, inspiration, intuition, effervescence and by that all encompassing word, ecstasy. When we experience the state of ecstasy it is unlike any other pleasurable experience we can encounter. Joy recharges us with the universe-balanced energy in the amount needed for our next task. When we do not have joy and/or happiness in our work, it becomes laborious and we get extremely fatigue from the wasted energy expended. The greater the joy within our consciousness, the greater the force of the recharge of thought-energy within us.

The following is an inspirational poem that has a very powerful message written by Walter Russell in his book titled, _The Divine Iliad:_

As the dawn telleth the coming of the new day:
I turn my eyes to the morning and purge myself in the purity
of the dawn.
My soul quicketh with the beauty of the dawn.
Today is, and will be.
Yesterday was, and has been.
My yesterday is what I made it. I see it in memory, perfect
or imperfect.
My today is what I will to make it. I will to make it perfect.
I have the power to build the day or to rend the day.
The day will be of my making; either perfect or imperfect,

good or bad as I choose to live it in spirit or in flesh, on the mountain top or earthbound.

If I rend the day I build ten other days, mayhap ten times ten, to undo the rending.

If I build the day I will have lived the day to the glory of the One in the fulfillment of that part of His purpose which is mine to fulfill.

So that I may meet the day with knowledge to build the day I will look into my soul while it is yet dawn, before the morning breaketh.

These are the words with which I greet the day.

These are the words of the morning.

This is the spirit of the dawn.

To me the universe is an open book.

I need not to learn. I know.

I see the unseen form the mountaintop.

I hear the music of the spheres.

I know the transcendent joy creation.

Immortality is mine.

I will earn immortality.

Mine is the power to give immortality, I shall not deny that which shall give immortality to those who dwell in darkness and who reach out for the light.

I will reach out my hand into the darkness and lead him that asketh into the light.

I will keep my body charged with energy for the fulfillment of my purpose, in accord with that which is commanded of me.

The power of the dynamic universe is behind my thinking.

Power is mine to give by the wayside.

I will not deny to any man who asketh the power which is mine to give.

I have no limitations. Unlimited power is mine within that which is universal.

I will do today that which is of today and pay no heed to the tomorrow, nor waste regrets on that which was yesterday.

My day shall be filled to overflowing, yet shall I not haste the day; nor shall I waste the day.

Those things which I must do I shall desire to do.

Courtesy will be in my heart to give to all.

My joy will be in serving.

My power will be in thinking true.

My power will be in knowing.

My power will be in humility.

The taint of arrogance will I not know.

That which is I, will I keep within the shadow of the beautiful temple of modesty, but my doings will I send forth into the light that all may see; therefore, must my doings be true.

Force will I meet with gentleness, impatience with patience.

Truth will guide my footsteps through tortuous paths and lead me to the glory of the day's golden evening.

I will sing the day through with a glad song, that the problems of the day shall be as chaff before the wind and that others may harken to my song and be quickened.

My countenance shall reflect the spirit within me, that all may see.

Blessed be the new day which descendeth upon me. I greet thee, O day. I cross thy threshold with joy and thanksgiving.

Oh! What a beautiful magnificent piece that we all can learn and benefit from, please read it with and open mind and heart so that we may grow strongly individually, as well as collectively. When reading the above it will remind you to let go of the past so you can live in the here now and to forgive yourself as well as others. Always, do something beautiful and great for the most wonderful person in the world – "YOU." Learn to truly love, enjoy and appreciate who you are and age gracefully by avoiding negative messages about yourself and aging. Also, I mandate that you know, remember and accept that the greatest of all knowledge is knowledge of self.

In addition, I am offering my following *W*ardisms on this subject of "SELF," please use your God given senses to understand and use them for your personal improvement:

Do not walk around in a trance; get in
balance and take your righteous stance.

W

Do not settle for being a copycat and
bend your back, always express your
creativity and keep your originality intact.

W

When you have the need, you must plant
the seed, then you will succeed.

W

When you are depressed and/or oppressed
you allow yourself to be suppressed and you
cannot truly express.

W

You must recognize that you are a divine
spiritual being, manifesting in a human form
wearing your skin to cover your divinity.

W

You know you have arrived when you can
say, "I am a citizen of this marvelous
beautiful vast majestic universal place
and a very proud spiritual being with membership in good standing of a transparent race."

Do not depend on another person to revive you;
you may not survive, so always look alive.

The more I learn about me, the more I become
to be and know about thee.

Use your mind, be kind and you will not get left
behind.

Always be your own leader, as well as an advocate
reader, then you will not have to seek membership
in a group as a follower.

I am the master of my fate, so I need not
lie, steal, hate or fall for the illegal bate.

Why work in vain, constant being in pain
and never realize any substantial gain.

Do not commit the old proverbial sin
by getting comfortable in your skin
forgetting that it begins from within.

If only your physical body represents your life
body of work, then you are poorly represented.

When you have peace within, you always win.

W

When you are gentle, kind and true to yourself,
you are the same to everyone else.

W

You win in the end because there is no sin to
overcome.

W

Always be a man/woman with a plan, it will
keep you from burying your head in the sand.

W

Do not focus on getting applauds or accolades
from others to validate your existence.

W

In essence, I am thee - humanly expressing me
to be free.

W

Always speak your truth very plain and simple
do not complain, take the opportunity to explain,
then you will not feel any shame.

W

Do not just sit on a pine; it is your time to shine,
get up and get in line, use your mine productively,
then you will be fine.

W

The human flesh houses our essence, do not
get it twisted with some other mess.

W

Your message of truth must be unchanged,
let it always remain the same.

W

He is he.
She is she.
I am me.
We all are trying to be like thee.

W

We are born uniquely unto ourselves, but die
trying to imitate others and still do not show love to
our brothers.

W

If you find yourself getting behind in your affairs,
just be kind to yourself and interact with persons
of like mind, then you will not think you are alone
blowing chaff in the wind.

W

Just because you are physically strong does
not give you the right to harm, hurt or treat
another person wrong.

W

Let your life be a shinning example for others
to duplicate and they can be a happy camper.

W

Live up to your name and do not play any silly
games that would make you feel ashamed.

W

It will be nice to say, "I did not fret," I did it
my way with no regrets.

W

As we age we should lose our rage and enjoy
being a sage on life's stage.

W

When your sanity is healthy, you will not
have to worry about your vanity.

You will always have your opinion, but
when you know your true mission, you
will make the right decision.

Know the essence of yourself, not what
someone would like for you to express.

When you have that "IT" whatever "IT" is,
you must allow that "IT" to manifest to its
fullness without a hitch in your niche.

Do not stay in your cage, and be in rage,
just become of age, and be a great sage.

We are so afraid to be original that we
settle for being a copy and then mope
about it.

Make sure you fought and sought to
achieve your dreams, so they will not
be an afterthought.

Every woman and man should always
have a good backup plan to maintain
his or her stance.

Aging gracefully made me a sagacious
person and gave me peace of mind, now
I can give praise.

It is nice to say, "I am free of all my debts
having lost very few bets and never been
in any real mess."

W

When meeting others always impart wisdom
to them, so you are able to depart gracefully and
peacefully without any anger, hate or
misunderstanding.

W

If you have a desire to do good no one has to
light your inner fire.

W

Stay in your place and monitor your pace,
then you will truly win life's race.

W

Do no let your life story be news that you did not
want reviewed.

W

Find your quest and do not be stressed dealing in
other folks' mess.

W

You only have yourself to blame if you end up in
life's hall of shame rather than life's hall of fame.

I AM TO DO WHAT I AM HERE TO DO

2
LIFE

We were created by our Almighty Divine Supreme Creator and brought forth in a human form through our parents to express our divine inheritance. We come forth to fulfill our destiny in this place in time and space, called earth, by expressing our individuality and to live out our life experiences until we complete our life journey. After we have completed this life journey, we will then transition into another place in time and space, commonly called death.

The purpose of life is to live it fully and abundantly. In addition, the Almighty Divine Creator gave us life for the purpose of expression. When we observe nature in its beautiful magnificence creation, we see the flower expresses itself through the beauty of its color, bloom and smell. The tree expresses itself in an upright position, its smiling leaves, shaking branches and sometimes hanging fruit. The lark expresses itself in its unique laughter and song. The sea expresses itself in its massive size by giving to the oceans, rivers and lakes in a very gentle calming manner. Men and women express themselves according to their idealistic visions and thoughts of nature. Therefore, it is important for men to be proud of their masculinity and women to be proud of their femininity, while a child remains childlike and progresses naturally into adulthood. We must accept and respect the fact that we are a child once, a man or woman once and a corpse once, by accepting these three stages we behave according to nature;

because that is the way nature planned it. We marvel at the innocence of how children prance and giggle, while men and women are dignified and serious in their pursuit of life and a corpse rest peacefully. Therefore, we must always remain serious about living our life experiences and stop building mental prisons for ourselves, occupying them and accepting the false premise of being mentally incarcerated for life. There should come a time in all our lives that we must humble ourselves and know we are earthly inhabitants of this vast beautiful majestic universe and the only request of us is to be respectful, kind and loving to our earthly neighbors. Further, we must know that we are here to be the keepers and protectors of humanity, as well as to learn what our individual plights are, because everyone has his or her place. Teachers must teach; doctors must cure; lawyers must defend; comedians must amuse, etc. It does not matter the position one may hold in life, we still must respect each other's individuality and each other's space.

Also, the ultimate purpose of living out our life's experiences is to seek, know and be the Almighty Divine Supreme Creator in essence. After all we are made in the image and likeness of our Creator as stated in Genesis 1: 26 - 27:

> And God said, Let us make man in our image, after
> our likeness: and let them have dominion over the
> fish of the sea, and over the fowl of the air, and
> over the cattle, and over all the earth, and over
> every creeping thing that creepeth upon earth.
> So God created man in his own image, in the image
> God created he him; male and female created he them.
>   -The King James Version

There is only one way to seek, know and be the Creator, by knowing and living the universal law of love. Humankind violates natural laws of the universe when they do not know the basic understanding of the Creator's ways and processes. The principle that underlies all natural law is love, which is better understood by using the three words, *"Rhythmic Balance Interchange."* The meaning of rhythmic balance interchange is equal giving for equal regiving and not receiving, because every pair of opposites in life is balanced equally, even unto death. By way of an example, what you plant in the ground is equal to that which comes out of the ground, if you plant watermelon seeds you do not get cantaloupes, you get watermelons. By showing love, kindness and righteousness toward one another, we are modeling, nurturing and living by that old principle that says, "Love and treat your neighbor as yourself." By allowing your life to be governed by this principle means sowing the seeds and the deeds of justice, which will grow into the kind of world intended for all of us by our Creator. When these good seeds are nourished by deeds of love and justice, then they will gradually take root and flourish throughout the world for everyone to enjoy. When we practice this kind of thinking throughout our lives, it becomes deeper and stronger to be past on to generations to come. Just think if the basis tenet of all organizations/institutions (i.e., churches, sororities, fraternities, social clubs, etc.) would subscribe to the aforementioned how wonderful, peaceful and beautiful the world would be for us to live in. Also, religious denominational loyalties and political partisanship should demand truthfulness and just actions for all humankind. We must avoid being around difficult people it helps to reduce stress. When we consistently think positive, speaking kind words and consistently do good deeds, we will transform our society and ultimately the world by sowing seeds of truth, love and mercy. Furthermore, if these good deeds are sown lovingly, courageously and willingly they will change this world to a world of peace, love and righteousness. Then we will live together in a world filled with peace and harmony, in a state of ecstasy.

It has been said that one must lose his or her life to find it. When we applied this concept in meditation, it means that he or she must lose (forget) his or her mortal body in order to become aware of his or her immortality. This is what happens when we seek the light of self-illumination in our eternal selves. We can only reach the great glory of existence by mind-awareness, as well as attain supreme heights, which come slowly through the desire to talk with the Almighty Divine Supreme Creator. There is no other way. For instance, if you desired to talk to the President of the United States, your mind would be centered on the reason why you desired to talk to him. Exactly the same procedure takes place when you wish to talk with the Creator, your mind must be centered on your desire. You cannot possibly think of other things, nor should your thoughts wander aimlessly. You must silence yourself and firmly concentrate on your desire by breathing and speaking your desire softly; then allow it to be written in your heart wordlessly. Your desire does not need to have a definite objective; you might just want to dwell in the love nature of your self with the Creator.

We must begin to think of our life as apart of the whole universal family and not just of ourselves along. Dr. Wayne W. Dyer said, "Intention is a force in the universe, and everything and everyone is connected to this invisible force." When we elevate our consciousness to the level of being fully aware of ourselves as a universal presence and a universal being, rather than thinking of ourselves as a body with a name, address and personality, then our living become more whole and complete. This is the way we should think and live out our life experiences. When we think of our life experience as one individual unit of creation, we put that one unit struggling for survival and for self-interest among countless other individual units. We must become aware that each person is interdependent on one another for happiness and survival since all living creatures in the universe is a dynamic extension of itself. By working in unity, we will not only survive but live an abundantly and ecstatically life experience. In addition, we will become aware of who we are and what we are and know our true purpose on this earth. By not thinking this way, we weaken our desires and become self-centered and the world will not enrich us with its glory or its bounty, because we are not enriching it. When our desires are for the whole (all persons), then we are stronger together and our life experiences are filled with peace, love, joy and much happiness. Everything in nature that is strong and substantial is simple; complexity tends to always weaken things. Notice in our life experience, our business, our home and especially our thinking are strong and substantial when simple. When life seems so complex and we have decisions to make because of these complexities, remember this one thing; we have only one simple decision to make at that very moment, yes only one. The next decision has not yet presented itself. The one decision we should make is that we shall do in love only that which makes us loved. This means the decision must be made in love with lovable intentions, so that everyone involved loves the outcome. The most important decision to make is to find true happiness for yourself and ultimately give happiness to humankind. Complexity is the beginning of the undermining of the structure that it is founded upon. In our life experiences, we can achieve any height of power we desire if we do not allow ourselves to be handicapped by the lack of knowledge because of doubts, fears, pessimism and any other negative effects to retard our thinking and/or growth. The Honorable Elijah Muhammad said, "When God created the universe from nothing, he destroyed the impossible." We should not have to constantly try to figure out everything, but just live a peaceful loving happy life with one another. We have made our life experience so complex that we lose sight of why we are traveling this life journey. Certainly it is not for the three meals a day, a car to ride in and/or a bed to sleep in as most individuals think. Our greatest purpose is to know our Almighty Divine Supreme Creator and the manifestation of its presence through each of us in human form here on earth. When we realize and accept this reality it will be a glorious wonderful world to live out our life experiences with one another in harmony.

We must know that life is to be lived and to be enjoyed abundantly and fully so we may receive its bounties and live in a state of ecstasy. In order to live life fully and abundantly, we must learn and practice the law of reciprocity. The law of reciprocity means to give so that we may receive in like measure, as well as to do unto to others, as we would have them do unto us. This should be apart of all men and women understanding, acceptance and spiritual enlightenment. Living our life experiences are akin to taking classes in school (it can be called the school of life), some of us are ahead of others in our spiritual learning (enlightenment). It is each of our responsibility to grow, respect and protect humankind equally as we do ourselves. This should be tantamount to striving toward receiving a letter grade of "A" in class from the school of life. Life is just learning the righteous way to live our individual life experiences. Edwin Markham said, "In vain do we build the city if we do not first build the man."

It must become apart of our daily living to practice the love principle of giving instead of taking from our fellow person. We must teach our children at a very young age whatever they do to another they are doing to themselves. That should be the very first principle they are taught pertaining to morality and character. When children learn this principle, they will show love, respect and kindness toward each other and hold true to the following quotation from The Message of the Divine Iliad:

> Serve first thy brother. Hurt first thyself rather than thy neighbor. Gain naught from him unbalanced by thy giving. Protect thou the weak with thy strength, for if thou use thy strength against him his weakness will prevail against thee, and thy strength will avail thee naught.

We must teach our children that they are hurting themselves when they hurt another person physically or speak unkind words to them. They must know that this is a natural law and then universal knowledge will become habitual to them. Failure to teach our children could result in what Adolf Hitler stated, "Give me a generation of children and I will give you another world of men who will be like me." The habit of thinking in patterns becomes traditional, then automatic. Teach a child in the right way he or she should live their life experience and then he or she might not stray along the way. Also, let us teach our children how to maintain and show love in their lives filled with harmony and let it be manifested in their common speech. Then they will be at peace with themselves and others as they reside in a peaceful world. We must be a shining example in our children lives by first being gentle, second being frugal and third being humble. This will teach them how to put others before themselves. Someone once said, "Be gentle and you can be bold, be frugal and you can be liberal, avoid putting yourself before others and you can become a leader of men." Our children are our future leaders, so it is important that we teach, guide and direct them on how to navigate their young lives on a righteous path. Parenting skills will be discussed in greater detail in Chapter 3, subtitle "Parenting."

We must be opened and receptive to attain non-traditional knowledge. The more knowledge one attains, the easier and happier one's life experience becomes because he or she knows how to meet and greet life. For example, if you were not familiar with the streets of Chicago and its traffic laws it would be quite difficult navigating to your destination; whereas one with knowledge of how to get around the city can travel all over with little ease. Likewise, our life experiences have traffic laws for everyone to obey. The greatest of these is the one law of balance. We must learn how to balance our interchange in every phase of our life experiences. If we have an unbalanced/unfair interchange, it causes a bad effect. We must stop allowing our business affairs and social interactions with others end up in conflict and/or in trouble dealings. Remember, we cause bad effects through unbalanced/unfair interchangings. Conversely, balanced/fair transactions cause good effects. Further, we frequently ask the question,

"Why do I have so much bad luck and draw negative thinking people into my life experience?" Well the answer is quite simple it is like looking through a crystal ball, in that without balance, fairness and order; we will unequivocally experience unbalance, unfairness and disorder in our life experiences.

When something is balanced, it will move without losing its balance, which is a natural law. That is true of planets floating in its orbit, as well as it is of an individual who must maintain his or her balance to walk correctly. Everything in the universe must be balanced and orderly, if not it will be unbalanced and in disorder. Our life experiences are like that, in that it is either balanced and orderly or unbalanced and disorderly. Our physical actions always reflect our mental thinking; it cannot be otherwise. Even though we may have the same thoughts but we do not have the same outcome about them. What we do is reflected in our actions; what we think is reflected in our face. In our life experiences, our actions are the result of the image we think, whatever the form, it is our thought-form. Remember, we think only that which we know, image or desire. On the other hand, we can only create, express or give out what we know. Our power lies in knowledge; our ability to express that power lies in what knowledge we are aware of consciously. Knowledge will build a stable life for us whereas ignorance can wreck our lives. Knowledge means ideas and balance/fair thinking means the power to think an idea into balanced. Effect is the perfect image of that idea it caused.

During our life experiences, we must learn the lesson of how to live in love, unity, peace and harmony with all humankind. We can only achieve this when every human transaction is a balanced transaction and know this is a natural law. We constantly hear, "The family that prays together, stays together." Let the communities pray together so they will stay together and foster love, unity, peace and harmony. Then it will spread naturally to our towns, to our countries and throughout our world. Once we have a world built on love, unity, peace and harmony, it is easy to see what good will exist throughout the world. Most notably, no more wars. Because, we would have rid our minds of hatred, greed, jealousy, as well as the other seven deadly sins. The seven deadly sins have had an enormous impact on the moral compass of the world. There are those who argue that they have a greater significance in morality than the Ten Commandments. It is believed that The Seven Deadly Sins are those transgressions that are fatal to our spiritual progress, they are:

1. *Lust* is usually thought of as excessive thoughts or desires of a sexual nature. Lust can lead to sexual or sociological compulsions and/or transgressions including, but not limited to: sexual addictions, fornication, adultery, bestiality, rape, perversion and incest. One having an inordinate craving for the pleasure of the body.

2. *Gluttony* is the over-indulgence and over-consumption of anything to the point of waste, having an inordinate desire to consume more than that which one requires.

3. *Greed* is like lust and gluttony, a sin of excess. Generally, greed is applied to the acquisition of wealth. Greedy behavior includes being disloyal, deliberate betrayal, treason for personal gain, theft, manipulation of authority, etc.

4. *Sloth* is the failure to utilize one's God given talents and/or gifts.

5. *Wrath* also known as anger or rage. It is described as inordinate and uncontrolled feelings of hatred and anger. These feelings can manifest as vehement denial of the truth to self, as well as others. One may desire to seek revenge outside of the workings of the justice system by doing harm to others.

6. *Envy* is characterized by an insatiable desire of resenting that another person has something they perceive themselves as lacking and wishing the other person to be de-

prived of it.

7. *Pride* is the desire to be more important or attractive than others, failing to acknowledge the good work of others. Having an excessive belief in one's own abilities that interferes with the individual's recognition of the grace of God. Pride is also known as vanity.

If we were to live our life experiences without violating any of the above-discussed deadly sins, this would be a beautiful, wonderful world filled with love, unity, peace, harmony, joy, kindness and happiness to all humankind. We will be able to show and give supreme respect to everything and everyone by acknowledging that the Almighty Divine Supreme Creator created all Creation. It will become second nature for us to treat all our neighbors with that all-encompassing love by helping and protecting them in a time of need.

Furthermore, we should always be willing to speak out against any wrong and/or negative action that we witness against our neighbor(s). We must endeavor to love everyone and take sides against all injustices and any kind of mistreatment against anyone. When we see a small group of elites taking advantage of the downtrodden for their own personal gain, we should get extremely angry and do whatever we can to bring matters in balance. Our anger, outrage and righteous indignation must remain focused on the wrong perpetrated and not to harm any particular group or person, but on the unjust policies and/or practices. We have heard several times that old age brings about wisdom, which means that wisdom is the result of many life experiences. If the cause of all the blessings of the world had to be answered in one word, that one word should be balance. Conversely, the one-word answer to the world's entire ills would be unbalance. Also, it is important to know that every person determines his/her own destiny by what he/she thinks and do during his or her life experience. We become what we want to be only through our thoughts, actions, and/or inactions. Our thoughts must be of high measure to achieve our greatness. In addition, we must be humble throughout our quest for greatness and know the quality of humility is what gives us warm-heartedness, kindness and the temperament of spiritual strength un-matched by any other. Consider this question, "What would you do if you knew you could not fail?" Life is a lifetime experiment in try-ing to find our way and place in it. It is full of comedy, tragedy and many other manifested problems that we are confronted with all the time. Our greatest challenge is to confront these life problems head on by identifying them and then resolve them. We must develop a living philosophy and/or paradigm that will allow us to face all our problems and rise above them with joy rather than sadness, hatred or anger. Sadness, hatred and anger are luxuries we cannot afford; they distort our perception, insight and perspective about life. We can be-come stronger as a result of our life experiences and accept them as important life lessons learned. Do not deal with your problem from a point of weakness, grief, pleading or supplication, it could create a long life of continuous unhappiness. Further, they can cause men-tal, physical, emotional and spiritual tension, stress and depression. Also, if you encounter a problem with a person, compromising is not necessary the best way to resolve the conflict; because you might be tempted to cure a wrong with a wrong. But, do not live in the past and allow your bad past negative life experiences dictate your future; in other words, do not let your past hold your future in hostage. Every past action is by choice and once you accept that everything happen to you as a child was part of your destiny, then it should be easy for you to get over it. The true evidence of that statement is the fact that it did happen. However, now it is over, it is gone, so let it be gone and not resurrect it mentally. You cannot bring back gone or catch gone, "it is gone;" in other words, "you cannot un-ring the bell," so let it be gone by releasing it and letting it go so you may move forward living a peaceful happy life. The best way to resolve a problem is to intelli-gently meet the challenge. This way lessen the tension and allow you to focus your energy on the problem so you are able to derive at the best solution. Ultimately, you must resolve your problem so you may have peace of mind and harmony in your life experience. Without a successful solution, you will experience unhappiness and your unhappiness cannot possibly co-exist with happiness. I am reminded of the following lesson a professor shared with his philosophy class on life, he said:

> When things in your life seem almost too much to handle, when twenty-four hours in a day are not enough, remember the mayonnaise jar and the two glasses of wine...
>
> The professor stood before his philosophy class and had some items in front of him. When the class began, wordlessly, he picked up a very large and empty mayonnaise jar and proceeded to fill it with golf balls. He then asked the students if the jar was full. They agreed that it was.
>
> The professor then picked up a box of pebbles and poured them into the jar. He shook the jar lightly. The pebbles rolled into the open areas between the golf balls. He then asked the students again if the jar was full. They agreed it was. The professor next picked a box of sand and poured it into the jar. Of course, the sand filled up everything else. He asked once more if the jar was full. The students responded with an unanimous "yes."
>
> The professor then produced two glasses of wine from under the table and poured the entire contents into the jar, effectively filling the empty space between the sand. The students laughed.
>
> "Now," said the professor, as the laughter subsided, "I want you to recognize that this jar represents your life. The golf balls are the important things; your family, your children, your health, your friends, and favorite passions; things that if everything else was lost and only they remained, your

life would be full."

The pebbles are the other things that matter; like your job, your house, and you car. The sand is everything else; the small stuff.

"If you put the sand into the jar first," he continued, "there is no room for the pebbles or the golf balls. The same goes for life. If you spend all your time and energy on the small stuff, you will never have room for the things that are important to you."

"Pay attention to the things that are critical to your happiness. Play with your children. Take time to get medical checkups. Take your partner out to dinner... Play another eighteen-round-of-golf. One more run down the ski slope. There will always be time to clean the house and fix the disposal. Take care of the golf balls first; the things that really matter. Set your priorities. The rest is just sand."

One of the students raised her hand and inquired what the wine represented.

The professor smiled and said. "I'm glad you asked. It just goes to show you that no matter how full your life may seem, there's always room for a couple of glasses of wine with a friend."

I believe the aforementioned really embodies the essential characteristics of how we should pursue and live out our life experiences. As you move through your life experience, do not sweat the small insignificant stuff live your life fully and abundantly.

HEALTHY LIVING

Our mental, emotional, physical and spiritual health is vitally important to us in order to live a productive happy joyous life experience. It is incumbent upon us to make every effort to keep these above aspects well healed. Healing is an intimate and integrative process that encompasses every aspect of our being. It involves the harmonious alignment of the mental, emotional, physical and spiritual aspects of our being with the powerful life force within us. Joy is one of the greatest means to harmonize the healing power within us. Joy conquers, cleanses, energizes and renews the mind and body. In addition, joy opens the way for each of us to tap into the deeper levels of our being, whereby we are able to connect with our inner rhythm and our greater sense of wholeness. It is a vital part of the restorative process that integrates every aspect of our being and is a direct aid to healing. When we are healed we are made whole or sound and we are restored to a healthy state that frees us from any ailment. Also, being healed can free us from anything evil or anything distressful; it cleanses, purifies and makes us feel well (if we feel will, we will look and act will). It is said, "Healing comes on the wings of joy." Further it is stated, "A cheerful heart is good medicine, but a broken spirit dry up the bones." The body naturally response to ideas of health and healing, this is why we must feed and nurture our minds with ideas of joy that creates laughter, strength, vitality, energy and vigor. We must always feed our minds with good positive mind food daily. There is a saying, "That good laughter anesthetizes the body." We must learn it is healthy and lovely to laugh, studies have found that a good belly laugh a day may keep the doctor away. In 2005, a study conducted at the University of Maryland Medical Center showed that laughter helped relax blood vessels, linking it to healthier function and a possible decreased risk of heart attack. The study revealed the following:

> The endothelium has a powerful effect on blood vessel tone and regulates blood flow, and coagulation and blood thickening, and secretes chemical and other substances in response to wounds, infections or irritation. It also plays an important role in the development of cardiovascular disease. It is conceivable that laughing may be important to maintain a healthy endothelium, and reduce the risk of

cardiovascular disease, says principal investigator Michael Miller, M.D., director of preventive cardiology at the University of Maryland Medical School of Medicine. "At the very least, laughter offsets the impact of mental stress, which is harmful to the endothelium."

Also, other studies have found that laughter may lower blood pressure and increase the amount of disease-fighting cells found in the body. So, it is important that you incorporate enjoyable happy fun things that will bring plenty of laughter into your life, as well as into your daily activities. It is said, "Laughter is nectar for the soul."

We must not allow our senses to become susceptible to the various kinds of negative reporting that we are frequently bombarded with daily. We must counteract these negative influences by building within our consciousness thoughts and words of the healing power of joy. Joy lives as a dynamic sustaining force with inner radiance that is never changed by outer circumstances or outer appearances. It is good to begin each day with meditation, joy and thanksgiving and praise the universe for calling you to unlimited opportunities for growth, success and service. It is this divine force within us that brings constructive results by the use of our faculty of imagination. In addition, we must make a conscious effort to firmly know and wisely understand that the best way to enhance our own life is to do something great for others. Remember, we can best take care of ourselves by taking care of others; having a positive outlook on life; being kind to others and just *smile*. Someone said, "If you smile in the morning it fortifies you all day long." Also, there is a verse in a song by Charlie Chapman that says, "Smile though your heart is aching – smile though your heart is breaking." So just keep smiling; smiling will bring happiness and joy in your life experience. Try it, what do you have to lose; it will probably work for you too. Remember our life experiences are full of learned life lessons; the following life lessons may help you get through your life challenges:

- Life is not necessary fair, but it is good.
- When in doubt, do not give out; take the next step.
- Life is too short to waste time hating anyone.
- Your job will not take care of you when you are sick. Your friends and relatives will, so keep in touch.
- Avoid unnecessary headaches; pay off the balance on your credit card each month.
- You do not have to win every argument, learn to agree to disagree and not be disagreeable.
- Start saving for your retirement when you receive your first paycheck.
- Make peace with your past so it does not screw up your future.
- Do not compare your life experience with others; you have no idea what their life experience is like.
- If your relationship has to be secret, you should not be in it.
- Everything can change in the blink of an eye, but do not worry, God never blinks.
- It is not that serious, take a deep breath, it calms the mind.
- Let go of anything that is not useful, beautiful or joyful to you.
- When it comes to going after what you love in life, do not take no for an answer.
- Polish and use the special silverware, burn the candles, sleep on the nice sheets, wear the fancy lingerie; do not save them for a special occasion, today is special, tomorrow is not promise to you.
- No one is in charge of your happiness but you.
- Frame every life's so-called disappointment with these

words, "In five years will this matter?"

- Always forgive everyone, because love and hate cannot coexist.
- What other people think of you is none of your business.
- Time can heal almost everything, so give it time.
- However good or bad a situation is, it will inevitably change.
- Do not take yourself so seriously, no one else does.
- Always be receptive and open for miracles, they are waiting everywhere.
- God loves you because of who God is, not because of anything you did or did not do.
- Growing old beats the alternative of dying young.
- All that truly matters in the end is that you shared and received love.
- If we all were to threw our problems in a pile and saw everyone else's, we would rush to grab ours back (things are not as bad as they may appear).
- No matter how you feel, get up, dress up, show up and do something.
- Know that the best is yet to come.

The above listed life lessons are true and tried; in that they have been experienced for centuries by many people of different cultures in many countries throughout the world.

We must learn to change our perception and then we are able to change our reality. Everything in our life experiences are there as a direct result of our core beliefs. When we change these core beliefs, we are then able to experience an entirely new life filled with all the wonderful things it has to offer, as well as what we truly seek out of life. With the advent of the tremendous amount of discussion center around new health care reform, it is imperative that we take some personal initiatives to reform our thoughts and know that we can heal ourselves through self-healing methods/therapies. There are many wonderful alternative methods/therapies for self-healing; I encourage you to seek out them for your wellness along with conventional medicine. The body is the most amazedly beautiful phenomenal mechanism created by the Almighty Divine Supreme Creator, which was designed in most instances to heal itself. When we injure our bodies, it repairs itself just as it was designed to do by nature. Take for example, if we were to cut ourselves or break an arm, our bodies have the natural built in capacity to heal the cut and repair the break. Further, if we get an infection, our immune system removes the germs from our bodies and restores the damaged tissue. If we get a flu virus or a cold virus, the immune system removes them from our bodies. There is no question that Mother Nature gave us a built in mechanism to repair our bodies and restore our health. If we damage our bodies severely, such as in an auto accident, then the body's repair mechanism might need some outside assistance. The assistance could be surgery, suturing, stitches, antibiotics, physical therapy, etc. After these things are implemented, then the body's natural repair system does the rest of the important work; it heals us and restores our body to its proper health and state of wellness for years to come.

Dr. Phil Kearney developed the *Self-Healing In Inner Awareness* program, which has revealed some break-through information and concepts regarding healing our inner difficulties. His studies and clinical therapy have shown that the mind is designed by nature to heal itself, just like the body heals itself. Dr. Kearney says:

> Some portions of our mind can be hurt by uncomfortable life experiences, and this is much like getting a broken bone. Fortunately, however there are other portions of the mind that does not become injured. These particular portions of the mind are the healing parts of the inner mind. They are specifically designed by nature to automatically heal the entire mind, just like our immune system heals

the entire body. In addition, we now know that these areas within the inner mind heal our uncomfortable thoughts, feelings, memories and beliefs on a routine daily basis, and they do so in a specific manner.

Further, Dr. Kearney believes the healing portions of the mind are also taught how to naturally acquire additional healing knowledge while healing is ongoing. Also, the mind learns how to maintain that wonderful healing state for us in the future.

There are many self-healing methods available that we can use to heal our own bodies and maintain a state of wellness, here are the names and methodologies of just a few:

1. *Emotional Freedom Technique (EFT)* – This is a tapping technique that affects the energy flow in the meridians of the body. EFT is a technique of tapping on acupuncture points to unravel negative emotions, limiting beliefs and the emotion core of many physical diseases. Individuals experienced at using EFT typically report an 80% or greater success rate and often get rapid, safe and natural relief from their problems without any sophisticated training in over 50% of cases. EFT is quick, in minutes or hours you can unravel nagging issues that would otherwise take years of traditional counseling. It is something you can do on your own or with the help of an EFT practitioner. Some proven studies have shown that EFT gives relief for the following problems and/or concerns:
   - Anxiety about going to the dentist
   - Post traumatic stress disorder (including symptoms such as stress, unreasonable fears, panic attacks, nightmares and flashbacks)
   - Epileptic seizures in small children
   - Reducing blood clumping
   - Improving eyesight

- Losing weight
- Quitting smoking
- Eliminating fear of water
- Increasing test scores
- Improving sports performance
- Overcoming depression
- Dealing with memories of abuse
- Improving personal relationships
- And much more

2. Reflexology is another method use for self-healing; it is the physical act of applying pressure to the feet and hand with specific thumb, finger and hand techniques without the use of oil or lotion. It is based on a system of zones and reflex areas that reflect an image of the body on the feet and hands with a premise that such work effects a physical change to the body. Surely, you looked at a reflexology chart at some time or another and noticed the body is reflected on the feet and hands. It serves as a map for technique application to target health goals. For instances, the left foot or hand reflects the left side of the body and the right foot or hand the right side. The spine reflex area runs down the inside of the feet and hands with reflex areas for the arm and shoulder reflected toward the outside of the foot or hand. The toes and fingers mirror the head and neck, as well as the parts of the body they encase. The ball of the foot mirrors the chest and upper back in addition to the heart and lungs. Also, halfway down the foot at the base of the long bones of the foot is represented the waistline of the body. The parts of the body above the waistline are mirrored above this line and those below represented below the waistline. Reflex areas above this line reflect internal organs lying above the body's waistline while those below

the waistline are mirrored below this line. In generally, the benefits of reflexology have to do with the reduction of stress. Because the feet and hands help set tension level for the rest of the body, they are an easy way to interrupt the stress signal and reset homeostasis (the body's equilibrium). However, there are further scientific studies needed in order to come to some definite benefits of reflexology in regard to illness and disease. The benefits of reflexology include but not limited too:

- Relaxation
- Pain reduction
- Amelioration of symptoms for health concerns
- Rejuvenation of tired feet
- Improvement in blood flow
- Impact on physiological measures
- Beneficial for post-operative recovery and pain reduction
- Enhancement of medical care
- Adjunct to mental health care
- Complement to cancer care
- Easier birthing – delivery – post-partum recovery

To build reflexology into your life is easy to do while doing other activities. For instance, just put a foot roller under your desk or work your hands in your spare time. Be creative but be consistent, five minutes a day is worth more an hour once in awhile.

3. Another method for self-healing is <u>The System For Self Healing,</u> which was developed by Rev. Christina Lynn Whited. It can be used to treat many kinds of pre-existing conditions by enabling the body to rally its own defenses in a more efficient manner. It should be used at a minimum of two months on a daily routine to see results. It takes less than one minute and can fit into your busy schedule very

easily; it should be used twice daily, morning and night. As I have said throughout my writings, "our words have tremendous power" and it is no different here. Therefore, we must truly believe in a positive outcome in our healing process. Rev. Whited's instructions are as follow:

- Begin by actually squeezing each toe gently between the thumb and forefinger. Hold each squeeze for three seconds. You can do both feet at the same time.

- Gently scratch the arch of each foot, an area about 3 inches long by 1 inch wide, with the tips of your fingers for three seconds.

- Again using the fingertips and beginning at the ankles, draw imaginary lines up each side of the shinbone, to the knee, pressing lightly. Do this three times per leg.

- Next, rub the surface of the solar plexus in a circle ten times. This is the area above the navel and below the breastbone. This can be done on top of a layer of clothing or with soap in the shower.

- Again using the fingertips, gently tap the area at the front of the neck from the jaw to the collarbone, and from beneath one ear to the center of the throat. You can easily use both hands at once. Repeat this across the area three times.

- Lastly, placing the thumb at the base of each ear and the fingertips at the back of the head in the mid-line, draw the fingers, with light pressure at all times, forward along the skull until they are in front of the ears. Keep the thumbs in place to use as a pivot point, repeat this motion three times.

4. Tai chi is a self-healing Chinese exercise system that uses

slow, smooth body movements to achieve a state of relaxation of both body and mind. Researchers have found that intensive tai chi practice shows favorable effects on the promotion of balance control, flexibility, cardiovascular fitness and reduced the risk of falls in both healthy and elderly patients. Also, those recovering from chronic stroke, heart failure, high blood pressure, heart attacks, multiple sclerosis, Parkinson's and Alzheimer's benefit greatly. Tai chi's gentle, low impact improvements burn more calories than surfing and nearly as many as downhill skiing. A later study led by the same researchers conducting the review found that tai chi, compared to regular stretching, showed the ability to greatly reduce pain and improve overall physical and mental health in people over 60 with severe osteoarthritis of the knee. In addition, a pilot study, which has not been published in a peer-reviewed medical journal, has found preliminary evidence that tai chi may reduce the severity of diabetes. The five essentials qualities of tai chi are.

- Slowness – To develop awareness.
- Lightness – To make movement flow.
- Balance – To prevent body strain.
- Calmness – To maintain continuity.
- Clarity – To focus the mind.

5. Generally, the practice of acupuncture is considered an Eastern Wellness Practice. It is considered the art and practice of living well naturally; it offers no drugs, surgery, blood work, x-rays, MRI's or Cat Scans. Eastern medicine believes there is a spectrum of health services available, which begins with less aggressive and more conservative measures than those mentioned. Eastern Wellness Practices offer the following:

- Acupuncture
- Sports
- Pediatric
- Stress Relief Acupuncture
- Homeopathy
- Nutrition
- Constructive living
- Meaningful Life Therapy
- Exercise

6. Fasting is the last self-healing method I will discuss in the chapter, however I strongly suggest that you seek out additional alternative methods on your own. Fasting allows the body to heal itself; it is the process of not eating food for a specific period of time. However, people fast for a variety of reasons. Some religions encourage their members to fast for various circumstances. Some health professionals believe that a short-term fast can help clear the body of toxins that build up during the processes of digestion. Others use modified fasts as a way of identifying whether a person has sensitivities to certain foods. You should be mindful of the following before starting a fast:

- Talk with a doctor or a qualified health professional before starting a fast, in order to make sure your body will be able to handle fasting for a period of time.
- People with certain medical conditions or pregnant are generally advised not to fast, unless supervised by a physician.
- It is important to plan your daily activities carefully while fasting. Your body might not have enough energy to keep up with your normal routine.

- You might need to plan naps or other relaxing activities during the day.
- If you are not accustomed to fasting, consider a
modified fast by drinking juice or eating fruit, so
your body will still be getting some calories and nutrients.

It is believed that fasting intensifies healing as deep tissue and
tired organs are repaired rapidly. For fasting to heal illness, the body
must pull all of its resources toward cleansing and repairing by re-
moving appetite and reducing or stopping digestion. For example,
wounded animals will fast and not eat until after their injury or broken
bones have healed. When we eat cooked or processed food during our
sickness the body's immune system is denied the opportunity to oper-
ate at its fullness. By fasting the body scours for dead cells, damaged
tissues, fatty deposits, tumors and abscesses, which burned for food or
expelled as waste. Also, diseased cells are dissolved in a systematic
manner, thereby leaving healthy tissue. This results in amazing thor-
ough cleansing of the tubes, membranes and cellular structures. Inges-
tion of mucus-forming foods clogs the body's microscopic tubes and
membranes, all of which are the highway used by the immune system.
Fasting dissolves this internal mucus. While fasting it is common for
the nose, throat and ears to pass sticky mucus that is clogging the si-
nuses. It is said during fasting, a metamorphosis occurs, because the
body undergoes a tearing down and rebuilding of damaged materials.
Fasting is known for its ability to rejuvenate and give the body a more
youthful look. I mentioned earlier about how amazing and wonderful our bodies are; this further shows how we can go for long periods
without any outside source of energy (food) and remain healthy. This
also shows how the body is able to find internal fuel (food) without
damaging the function of the whole body system. David Frahm said,
"Somehow my sense of God's presence and my complete reliance
upon him are heightened when I'm fasting." What a wonderful mar-

velous body created by our Almighty Divine Supreme Creator that we so wonderfully possess.

The aforementioned is just a few self-healing methodologies available for our personal use. There are many co-factors that determine who gets sick and who does not according to Blair Justice, PhD., author of *Who Gets Sick*. Beliefs, moods and thoughts affect the mind/body in many ways. Dr. Justice believes, "Whatever gives us an increased sense of control – whether it is love, faith, or cognitive coping – seems to mobilize our self-healing systems." Successful recoveries through such mind/body control have allowed many to gain access to their inner self-healer throughout history and in the present day. However, I will hastily add and strongly suggest that you should consult with a physician first and/or a professional practitioner who specializes in the above-discussed methodologies and/or therapies. They are to be used in conjunction with, not in lieu of. However, I am asking and pleading with you to seek out other ways by thoroughly investigating and educating yourselves on the availability and the use of alternative medicines. You should remain grounded yet judicial in your resolve; you might find the results to be quite comforting. Know that everything has its rightful place at its proper time, up to and including conventional medicine. You might notice I called these alternative medicines, however, there are those, who no doubt, would call conventional medicine alternative medicine. Because they treat the symptom by issuing prescription drugs and performing surgery; whereas, the others treat the cause and concentrate on prevention. It is written in the Ancient Book, *Nei Jing* that, "The inferior physician treats, the superior physician teaches." Just be mindful that these suggestions should not be a replacement to good medical help and/or advice, it is your decision. Please make wise decisions by first conducting your own research for a better understanding. Remember there is no truth until you decide your own truth. In addition, make sure you become in tune with and learn to listen to your body, because your body talks to you. It will alert you when an aliment or illness occur, as well as reject what it does not need.

Before I conclude this topic on health, I would be extremely remiss if I did not discuss knowing the importance of your family health history, both physically and psychologically. It is worth taking the time to learn about your relatives' health physically and mentally. Former U.S. Surgeon General Richard H. Carmona said, "Knowing your Family history can save your life." You need to know if your mother, father, siblings, aunts, uncles and/or grandparents, as well as half-brothers and half-sisters (they too share some of your DNA) have ever suffered from any of the following:

- Diabetes
- Heart disease
- Depression
- Any mental health problems
- Any type cancer
- Type of allergies
- High blood pressure
- Kidney disease, etc.

Try to ascertain as much information as possible, up to and including what a particular relative died from and at what age. You should obtain this type information on as many of your family generations as possible. There are several ways to identify your family members who may be at risk, by knowing this information could keep from passing various diseases on to your children, such as:

- Discuss medical history at family gathering (a major holiday like Thanksgiving, etc. is a good opportunity)
- If possible, review family medical records
- Collect information that caused a major medical condition
- Review death certificates for cause of death

The primary reason for acquiring your family medical history is because you share their genes, environment, lifestyles and habits. Even if you do not have a history of a particular health problem in your family, you still could be at risk. Your personal medical history, lifestyle and other factors influence your chance of getting a disease. You cannot change your genes, but you can change unhealthy behaviors and reduce your risk of disease by eating a healthy diet, getting enough exercise and not smoking. Once you acquire your family medical history share it with your doctor, who can assess your disease risk. Your doctor may refer you to a specialist to determine whether you have an inherited form of disease that is passed on from generation to generation. Also, genetic testing may help to determine if you or any of your family members are at risk. Once again, it cannot be overly emphasized when you adopt a healthier lifestyle, you can greatly reduce your risk for disease that run in your family.

Also, your family history can predict risk of mental disorder to determine if you are predispose to diseases such as, anxiety, depression, schizophrenia, bipolar, alcoholism and drug abuse. Barry J. Miline and colleagues at the University of Auckland, Dunedin, New Zealand research showed that a person's family history not only reveals their risk for condition such as, anxiety, depression, alcoholism and drug abuse. Also, the research revealed that it might predict the course of the illness and prognosis. In addition their research revealed the following:

> In general, we found that associations showed a consistent direction of effect across all four disorders:
>> 1. Family history was associated with the presence versus absence of disorder for all four disorders types.
>> 2. Family history was associated with a recurrent course for all four disorders (but not significantly depressed women).
>> 3. Family history was associated with worse impair-

ment for all four disorders (but not significantly for depression and drug dependence).

4. Family history was associated with greater service use for all four disorders (but not significantly for anxiety disorders).

The above research was published in the July 2009 issue of the journal *Archives of General Psychiatry*. This study is important because it dealt with the genetic forms of a disorder and provides information for doctors treating patients with psychiatric disorders. The research included 981 residents of Dunedin, New Zealand, who were enrolled at age 3 and followed until they were age 32. The researchers acquired data on the participants' biological parents, grandparents and siblings.

I encourage all who read this book to please share this information with your family, friends and even your foes, and to unquestionably telling them that they have an ultimate responsibility to be healthy physically, mentally, spiritually and emotionally. You need to further impress upon them by being healthy in all of the aforementioned areas; they will be able to think clearer and approach living their life experience in a more harmonious, loving, joyous, peaceful and kind ways. When you are healthy you will see everything differently, in a more positive light, whereby everything around you change for the better. I recall the following quote by O. Carl Simonton, M.D. that sums up having complete health and wellness:

> The more I can love everything – the trees, the
> land, the water – my fellow men, women, and
> children – and myself, the more health I am
> going to experience and the more of my real
> self I am going to be.

Our life experience is eternal in quality, it lives, moves, evolves in an unfolding process. Whatever we mentally see and spiritually comprehend, we may objectively experience because our life is not limited to any one experience. The invisible presence of the Almighty Divine Supreme Creator is the cause desiring self-expression through us; it is the insistent urge compelling us to continue to move forward. The eternal quality of humankind and of life rises up again and again to overcome doubt and fear to bring light into darkness and to open the blind eyes, the deaf ears and the closed minds. We must learn to adhere to the divine qualities of life, love and power by transcending the experience of the moment and enter into new and higher ways to live out our life experiences. Know that our life is the reflection of our internal belief systems, not our external circumstances. Do not take life so serious that you lose sight of all the beauty existing around you, learn to just relax, rejuvenate, energize yourself and enjoy your life experience abundantly. Most of all enjoy being able to express yourself in the beautiful healthy body that you have helped to create for yourself, now and for the rest of your life.

It is extremely important and part of our personal responsibility to do everything within our human power to live a long quality life (longevity has its place). In the book titled, *Blue Zone*, authored by Dan Buettner, he wrote that the island of Okinawa, Japan has the most people to live to celebrate their 100 birthdays, in their communities they are highly honored and called centenarians. He said: "Somehow Okinawans managed to reach the age 100 at a rate up to three times higher than that of Americans. They suffered a fifth the rate of heart disease, and lived about seven good years longer."

The question is what do they contribute to their secrets toward good health and a long life? The following Okinawa's longevity lessons may serve as an aid to help us understand how to live a good long quality happy peaceful life:

1. *Ikigai* is a primary way of life with the Okinawain's centenarian, which is defined, "the reason to wake up in the morning." A centenarian is someone who reaches the age of 100 and older, but a super centenarian is a person aged

110 and higher. A nonagenarian is a person in his or her 90s. The centenarian states that ikigai is having a sense of purpose for waking up in the morning and knowing that beauty is within and all around you. In addition, ikigai is not worrying so much about your own problems; the centenarians would say, "Sometimes you can best take care of yourself by taking care of others." They added, "Eat your vegetables, have a positive outlook, be kind to people and smile." Their strong sense of purpose may act as a buffer against stress and help reduce their chance of suffering from Alzheimer's disease, arthritis and stroke. They do not believe in living in the past. When there is a sudden loss of a person's traditional role it tends to have a measurable effect on mortality. We see this especially among teachers, firemen, policemen, etc. who die very soon after they quit working; because they loss their sense of purpose. Everyone should craft a personal mission statement with a sense of purpose. Your mission statement for living should include why you get up in the morning; what you are passionate about; how you enjoy using your talent(s) and what is truly important in your life. Also, find someone to whom you can communicate your life purpose, along with a plan for understanding it. It can be a spouse, a family member or a friend; it does not matter as long as it is someone who can help you honestly assess your plan and your successes. Add something new in your life, take up playing a musical instrument and/or learn a new language. Both of these activities are among the most powerful things you can do to preserve your mental sharpness.

2. *Diet* is one of the essential elements toward living a happy productive life. We are constantly inundated with what the best kind of diet for us through the electronic and print

media, which makes it very hard to make an intelligent decision. The older Okinawans have eaten a plant-based diet most of their lives. Their meals of stir-fried vegetables, sweet potatoes and tofu are high in nutrients and low in calories. Goya, with its antioxidants and compounds lower blood sugar. Goya is a melon that looks like a wart-covered cucumber. Also, mugwort is an intricate part of their daily diet. Mugwort is one species of the genus Artemisia, which contains the most powerful natural substance for fighting malaria. Recently, The World Health Organization made it a top priority for one form of Artemisia to be made available in developing countries. The Okinawan diet is rich foods made with soy, like tofu and miso soup. Flavonoids in tofu may help protect the heart and guard against cancer. Fermented soy foods contribute to a healthy intestinal ecology and offer even better nutritional benefits. Soy products that contain phytoestrogens are probably better than hormone supplements. Some researchers speculate that they may impart many of the benefits of estrogen without the cancer danger. Soy has the ability to lower the level of "bad" (LDL) cholesterol in the body and the potential to reduce the risk of heart disease. It is found in a wide variety of forms, from tofu, soymilk and soybeans in their pads. While centenarians Okinawans do eat some pork, it is traditionally reserved only for infrequent ceremonial occasions and eaten only in small amounts.

3. *Gardening* serve many purposes, one of which is quite oblivious, in that you are in control of what you plant, as well as what you are using to grew your corps, i.e. pesticides. Almost all Okinawan centenarians grow or at least once grew a garden. For them, it is a source of daily physi-

cal activity that exercises their bodies with a wide range of motion and helps reduce stress. It is also a near-constant source of fresh vegetables. Researchers have shown physical activity account for a gain of an extra couple of years added to one's life. Physical activity reduces heart disease, breast and colon cancer, as well as maintains a fairly normal body weight.

4. *Moai* – maintaining a social network; social connectedness. Moai roughly means "meeting for a common purpose," it originated as a means of the Okinawan financial support system. If anyone needed capital to buy a parcel of land or take care of an emergency, they would assist by pooling money together to help locally. Today the idea has expanded to become more of a social network, a ritualized vehicle for companionship. These safety nets lend financial and emotion support in times of need and give all their members the stress-shedding security of knowing that there is always someone there for them. It appears that all human beings feel that they need to belong to or connect to a social group in order to meet and get information and/or fellowship. Professor Lisa Berkman of Harvard University has investigated social connectedness and longevity. In one study, she looked at the impact of marital status, ties which friends and relatives, club membership, and level of volunteerism on how well older people aged. Over a nine-year period, she found that those with the most social connectedness lived longer. Higher social connectedness led to greater longevity. Those with the least social connectedness were between two and three times more likely to die during the nine-year period of the study than those with the most social connectedness. The type of social connectedness was not important in relation to longevity

– as long as there was connection. Even if a person does not have a spouse or a significant other, other forms of social connection could compensate for them. It is a belief that women live longer because they have superior social support networks compared to that of men.

5. *Enjoy the sunshine* – vitamin D, produced by the body when it is exposed on a regular basis to sunlight. It promotes stronger bones and healthier bodies. It appears that vitamin D is an important ingredient in the longevity recipe, because our skin manufactures it when it comes into contact with the sun. Without vitamin D, we increase our risk for nearly all age-related diseases including many types of cancer, high blood pressure, diabetes and even autoimmune diseases like MS (multiple sclerosis). Insufficient vitamin D markedly accelerates heart disease in kidney patients. When we do not receive enough vitamin D our bones become brittle, hip and leg muscles become weak and the chance of falling and breaking bones increase. Also, lack of vitamin D is associated with a host of problems, such as osteoporosis and heart disease; so it is important to make sure we get enough of this vital nutrient. Okinawans spend each day outside in the sun in order that they may receive optimal levels of vitamin D year-round.

6. *Stay active* – activity has always been associated with being healthy and living a long quality productive life. Older Okinawans are active walkers and gardeners. The Okinawans household has very little furniture; they eat their meals and relax on tatami mat on the floor. The fact that old people get up and down off the floor dozen times daily builds lower body strength and balance, which help protect against dangerous falls. Walking is an activity all successful centenarians did and do almost daily. It is free (just

purchase a good pair tennis shoes), easier on the joints than running, always accessible; you can be accompany by others. After a hard day, a walk can relieve stress; after a meal, it can aid digestion. There is a combination of four types of exercise that will keep the body balanced and strong for endurance. Activities like walking, hiking, swimming, and cycling improve the health of the cardiovascular system. For strength, lifting weights builds up and maintain muscles. For flexibility, stretching is good to keep limber. For balance, try standing on one leg for short periods of time, try Yoga or Tai chi. The above are the kinds of activities longevity experts have in mind when they talk about exercising for the long haul.

7. *Positive attitude* – having a positive attitude goes a long way in making your day pleasant and enjoyable, as well as enjoying the company of others. You must let go of past negative happenings you had in your life experience. Forgive and forget those who have wronged you, so you can move forward and live a happy peaceful life. Sometimes people are not aware they have wronged you, so they are living happy while you are holding on to the negative thoughts about them. A hardship-tempered attitude has endowed Okinawans with an affable smugness. They are able to let their difficult early years remain in the past while they enjoy today's simple pleasures of life. They have learned to be likable and to keep younger people in their company well into their old age.

The aforementioned living habits surely have contributed greatly to the Okinawa centenarians' longevity; obviously, we can learn from them how to increase our living habits. My greatest hope is that one day we will use preventive medicine to ward off and/or prevent any kind of ailment or disease, as oppose to receiving prescription medication to care for an ailment or disease. Beware that most medications prescribed by doctors have some kind of side effects, it is called "medical practice." Thomas Edison said: "The doctor of the future will give no medicine but will interest his patients in the care of the human frame, in diet, and in the cause and prevention of disease."

I want to add that meditation is vitally important in living a long happy productive life, as well as reading and listening to motivational and spiritual messages. Meditation provides us with a mechanism to step out of our self-focus and find true freedom, as well as to get in touch with our spiritual side. Regular meditation can allow us to slow down our minds and eliminate the incessant chatter in our heads. Also, meditation focuses concentration and allows us to see the world as it really is instead of how we imagine it to be. It sets up our day and helps us to realize that rushing, worrying and the urgency we give to so many things in our lives really are not so important. To meditate, create a space in your home that is quiet, not too hot or not too cold, not too dark or not too light. Furnish the space with a meditation cushion or chair. Establish a regular meditation schedule and try to meditate every day no matter what, but do not get stress out if you fail to do so. Start with 10 minutes a day and work up to 30 minutes a day. These are just some suggestive tips to aid you in meditating; however do whatever works for you, meditation does not have to be so rigid or so ritualistic to receive its benefits. It is to serve as mind food.

The following is one of the most powerful pieces ever written; every time I recite it to audiences I receive great ovations. It is believed that it was written in 1692; it was relevant then, as well as now. It is so meaningful that it has two names: *The Desiderata* (a Latin word meaning desire) and *The Master Message*, it is said that the author(s) is/are unknown:

Go placidly amid the noise and haste, and remember what

peace there may be in silence...

As far as possible, without surrender, be on good terms with all persons. Speak your truth quietly and clearly; and listen to others, even the dull and the ignorant; they too have their story. Avoid loud and aggressive persons; they are vexations to the spirit.

If you compare yourself with others, you may become bitter or vain, for always there will be greater and lesser persons than yourself. Enjoy your achievements as well as your plans. Keep interest in your own career, however humble; it is a real possession in the changing fortunes of time... Exercise caution in your business affairs, for the world is full of trickery. But let this not blind you to what virtue there is; many persons strive for high ideals, and everywhere life is full of heroism...

Be yourself. Especially do not feign affection. Neither be cynical about love; for in the face of all aridity and disenchantment, it is perennial as the grass...Take kindly the counsel of the years, gracefully surrendering the things of youth. But do not distress yourself with dark imaginings. Many fears are born of fatigue and loneliness.

Beyond a wholesome discipline, be gentle with yourself. You are a child of the universe no less than the trees and the stars; you have a right to be here. And whether or not it is clear to you, no doubt the universe is unfolding as it should. Therefore, be at peace with God, whatever you conceive him to be.

And whatever your labors and aspirations, in the noisy confusion of life, keep peace in your soul. With all its sham, drudgery and broken dreams, it is still a beautiful world. Be cheerful. Strive to be happy.

The above can be a personal mantra for us to live by in order to have a peaceful harmonious life experience. The following is one of my personal meditations and prayers that I wrote some years ago to frequently concentrate on and hold deeply in my conscious during my quiet time as well as other times; I will loudly utter the words to balance the energy around me (my magnetic field):

> *I am a divine being moving throughout my human life experience. I am gentle, kind and loving to others, as well as my surroundings and myself. I know, I must not be too hard or critical of myself because I fully accept my divine uniqueness. I desire, radiate, express and seek love, peace, victory, joy, happiness, kindness, understanding, knowledge to be enlightened, and all that is good and perfect and nothing that is not. So peace and patience be unto me as I stay and remain in balance while traveling throughout this beautiful, wonderful, vast, majestic life journey, giving and receiving all the blessing that the Almighty Divine Supreme Creator has bestowed upon me to bestow upon humankind, as well as to receive and live my divine life fully and abundantly. Show me my Father-Mother-God, the Almighty Divine Supreme Creator, what I should do to fulfill my purpose and to do my part; so that I may rejoice and be happy as I live and remain in a state of ecstasy.*

I wrote the aforementioned for myself, you can write your own meditation/prayer that will be pleasing, satisfying and comforting to your spiritual existence. In addition to the above mantras, I believe if you were to incorporate the following into your lifestyle you will be a calmer happy person as you have your being daily:

- Maintain a healthy lifestyle mentally, physically, spiritually and emotionally.
- Exercise regular (moderately).
- Spend time with like-minded friends.
- Practice giving something back.

- If you eat meat do so in moderation.
- When snacking try eating nuts, raw vegetables, fruit, oaks, etc.
- Eat light dinners.
- Add more plant food to your daily diet.
- Drink plenty of water.
- Get enough sleep daily.
- Get involved with doing something worthwhile.
- Explore new and interesting ideas within means.
- Just smile and love life immensely.
- Find a sanctuary and meditate often.

Healthy people throughout the world everywhere have faith. The simple act of worship is one of those subtly powerful habits that seem to improve our chances of having more good years; it does not matter if you are Christian, Buddhist, Hindu, Muslim, Jewish, etc. One thing appears to remain constant in all religions that there is one Supreme Being, no matter what name is given to identify, honor, glorify or praise. Studies have shown that attending religious service even as infrequently as once a month may make a difference in how long a person lives. The study in *the Journal of Health and Social Behavior* reported following 3,617 people for seven and half years and found that those who attended religious services at least once a month reduced their risk of death about a third. As a group, the attendees had a longer life expectancy, with an impact about as great as that of moderate physical activity. There is a belief that people who attend church are less likely to engage in harmful behaviors and more likely to take on healthful behaviors. Belonging to a religious community can foster larger and denser social networks. People who attend services may have higher self-esteem and self-worth because religion encourages positive expectation, which in turn can actually improve one's health. By adhering to a religion allow individuals to relinquish the stresses of everyday life to a higher power. Also, these individuals tend to follow a code of behavior that has been laid out before them by their religiosity's rituals and/or dogmas. They believe by following it that they will have peace of mind, whereby they will engage in "right living." They rationalize, if the day goes well perhaps I deserve it. Conversely, if the day goes poorly, it was out of my hands.

The aforementioned study was silent as to whether organized groups other than the church had the same results. I personally believe any well establish or an organized group with a righteous mission, objective and/or purpose will suffice. In addition, it is my belief that some religious services can be too rigid, too stern and too firm with their rituals and dogmas losing its luster, objective and primary purpose. I believe as long as you are meeting with people of like thinking, without confusion, but with loving positive vibrations and ideals to make the world better and to aid in helping their neighbors then the same goal is achieved. In the previously sited study conducted by Professor Lisa Berkman of Harvard University, under the discussion of Moia (maintaining a social network); she clearly indicated that close ties with relatives, family members, club membership and level of volunteerism contributed mightily to longevity. It is noted that the Okinawan centenarians met with a group of people for a mutual support network whom they had known their whole lives. Their purpose was to lend support to one another that might be in need of food, clothes, etc., up to and including financial support. Also they would use this time to catch up on the town gossip/news.

There is a raging debate on religion versus spirituality, in terms of their established meaning and what one purports to do compared to the other one. One can conclude that religion is spiritual and spirituality is religious; however it said that religion incorporates public rituals and organized doctrines. Whereas, on the other hand, it said that spirituality tends to be more personal and private. The word "religion," comes from the Latin word meaning to bind oneself, to commit oneself. The American Heritage Dictionary defines religion as (1) The expression of man's belief in and reverence for a superhuman power recognized as the creator and governor of the universe. (2) Any particular integrated system of this expression, (3) The spiritual or emotional attitude of one who recognizes the existence of a superhuman power or powers. (4) Any objective attended to or pursued with zeal or conscientious devotion. In the same dictionary, spirituality is defined, (1) The state, quality, or the fact of being spiritual. (2) Ecclesiastics collectively: the clergy; spirituality. (3) Something belonging to the church or to an ecclesiastic, as property or revenue. In comparison, many practitioners define "Spirituality" to mean: quiet, tranquil meditation, an unhurried, restful, low-stress lifestyle; as well as a philosophical life spent discussing spiritual things, like when Jesus might be coming back. Also, the spiritualists believe that any individual who works on spiritual self-development takes responsibility for their life and connects with the language of their soul. Then they automatically become a loving, expansive, healthy, happy and inspirational being who serves other in loving and inspiring ways. They say, " If we are 'at one' with ourselves, we are complete and 'at one' with the world. There is no need to harm, take, control, pillage or rob." Further, the spiritualists believe once we learn about the 'God within' we will know and accept ourselves as gorgeous, all loving and Divine beings. In Neville Goddard's book entitled, *Resurrection*, he translates the Deuteronomy passage as follows:

Hear O man (Human Being), made of the very substance of God: You and God are one and undivided! Man, the world, and all within it are conditioned states of the unconditioned one, God. You are this one; you are God, conditioned as man. All that you believe God to be, you are; but you will never know this to be true until you stop claiming it of another and recognize this seeming other to be yourself. God and man, spirit, matter, the formless and the formed, the creator and the creation, the cause and the effect, your Father and you are one. This one, in whom you live and move and have your being, is your *I am*, your unconditioned consciousness.

Once we know and accept the above quote, we will acknowl edge ourselves as miracles and shamelessly love and embrace ourselves. We will rid ourselves of the guilt, fear and lack of deservedness and only then, will we learn how to provide our own happiness and honor ourselves and make decisions and choices based on the truth of our soul. Because there is no truth until you decide your own truth. Knowing that we will always have love, success, happiness and glorious relationships in pure abundance and willing to share it with others particularly and the world in generally.

RELIGION

A group of social scientists studied 346 people representing a wide range of religious backgrounds in an attempt to clarify what is implied when individuals describe themselves as "spiritual, but not religious." They found that religiousness was associated with higher levels of interest in church attendance and commitment to orthodox beliefs. In contrast, they found that spirituality was associated with higher levels of interest in mysticism, experimentation with unorthodox beliefs, practices and having negative feelings toward both clergymen and churches. Most respondents in the study tried to integrate elements of religiousness and spirituality. Yet 19 percent of their sample constituted a separate category best described as "spiritual not religious." Compared with those who connected interest in private spirituality with membership in a public religious group, the "spiritual but not religious" group was less likely to: (1) Evaluate religiousness positively, (2) Engage in traditional forms of worship such as church attendance and prayer and (3) Engage in-group experiences related to spiritual growth. However, this same group was more likely to: (1) Be agnostic, (2) Characterize religiousness and spirituality as different and non-overlapping concepts, (3) Hold tradition beliefs and (4) Have had mystical experiences. Those who see themselves as "spiritual, but not religious" reject traditional organized religion as the sole or even the most valuable means of furthering their spiritual growth. Many have had negative experiences with churches or church leaders. For example, they may have perceived church leaders as more concerned with building an organization than promoting spirituality, as hypocritical or as narrow-minded. Some may have experienced various forms of emotional or sexual abuse.

The root for most "popular" religions is the same, in that the Old Testament covers Judaism, Christianity and Islam. If we would delve into most mythologies, we will clearly find similarities, recurring themes and morals. The virgin birth appears in many forms other than Christianity and for those of you who may think many of the biblical stories are unique, I assure you this is not the case. Do your own research and take no man's version. I believe that Christianity, Judaism, Islam, etc. have been stripped of the very meaning of their words. Because Jesus, Muhammad, Moses and the other great prophets have been made an exception to the rule rather than the rule to serve as examples for us to live our life experiences by. We find many individuals holding themselves out as reverends, right reverends, fathers, (which are nonbiblical titles) conveying textual re-do techniques through their homiletics that are described as "hermeneutics," yet missing the mark. Hermeneutics is the science and methodology of interpretation of Scripture text. Their interpretations, in some cases, are flawed, leave a lot to be desired and open to many unanswered questions, because of their misinterpretation, skip-over, inaccuracies, etc. There is a Italian proverb that says, "Every translator is a traitor."

Despite all the pomp and circumstance permeating the church today, the truth is that Jesus did not find an institution; he started a movement. Obery M. Hendricks, Jr., in his book entitled, *The Politics of Jesus (2006)*, stated:

> Jesus ordained no bishops, pastors, deacons, or trustees. He issued no ecclesiastical decrees, wrote no complicated doctrines, establish no churches, endorsed no religious hierarchies. Jesus simply taught the men and women who heeded his call to put their love for God into practice by loving their neighbors as themselves. All Jesus had was a movement, plain and simple, and all who followed him in his lifetime were not only his disciples, they were also partners in that movement.

We must take it upon ourselves to go into deep meditation and prayer coupled with conducting our own research and then unemotionally derives at our own prudent conclusion. Unfortunately, when it comes to religion and spirituality, too many of us are close-minded, which is truly sad because there is so much we can learn from one another. For example, most Native Americans have no word in their language for "religion," they believe spirituality or faith is something you supposed to experience every day, such as air. In reality no one has to preach air or proclaim its existence because every living thing requires it. We must come to the realization that spiritual air is natural, unable to be rejected or denied. Religious air is a construct of men and it is artificial. Even if religion did not exist spirituality would.

Since I am discussing religion, I feel lead to further discuss and draw some similarities on some of the world major religions. Primarily, because arguments/debates and wars have been fought and countless individuals have lost their lives over religion. I ask the question, *"for what reason(s)?"* There is no time or place in history that religious movements cannot be founded, they included religious practices, also local traditions and reforms. There are twelve classical world religions, which are most often included in history of world religion surveys and studied in world religions classes, they are: Baha'i, Buddhism, Christianity, Confucianism, Hinduism, Islam, Jainism, Judaism, Shinto, Sikhism Taoism and Zoroastrianism (some of these are referred to as the Abrahamic Religions). I will briefly discuss their practices, concepts and/or beliefs so it will become clearer why different faiths, expressions and disciplines exist. They wear the mask of their culture in order to speak to the people in a voice they can connect with. The following describes their doctrines, beliefs, teaching methods, practices and sacred leaders:

Baha'i – The Baha'i faith believes that there is one God who sends divine messengers to guide humanity throughout time, which is called Progressive revelation (Baha'i), it is different from the Christian belief of Progressive revelation (Christian). They believe in the divine knowledge and essence of Jesus, among other messengers such as Muhammad, Zoroaster and Moses. There interpretations vary, but the Baha'i Faith is sometimes considered an Abrahamic faith. The followers of the Baha'i Faith believe God, as do Christian, and recognize Jesus' teachings, but they have different views of the Trinity and divinity of Jesus. The Baha'is' view of prophets is that although they have both human and divine characteristics, they are not themselves God, but rather "divine manifestations." They also see the Trinity as symbolic where Jesus and the Holy Spirit are polished mirrors that reflect the pure light from God. In addition, they condemn polygamy, premarital sex and homosexual acts, while treating everyone, including homosexuals, with love, respect and dignity.

Buddhism – was founded in the fourth or fifth century B.C. in northern India by a man known traditionally as Siddhartha (meaning "he who has reached the goal") Gautama, the son of a warrior prince. Some scholars believe that he lived from 563 to 483 B.C., though his exact life span is uncertain. Troubled by the inevitability of suffering in human life, he left home from a pampered life at the age of 29 to wander as an ascetic, seeking religious insight and a solution to the struggles of human existence. He passed through many trials and practiced extreme self-denial. Finally, while meditating under the bodhi tree ("tree of perfect knowledge"), he reached enlightenment and taught his followers about his new spiritual understanding. Gautama's teachings differed from the Hindu faith prevalent in India at the time. Whereas in Hinduism, the Brahmin caste (a highly cultured and socially exclusive person) alone performed religious functions and attained the highest spiritual understanding, Gautama's beliefs were more egalitarian, accessible to all whom wished to be enlightened. At the core of his understanding were Four Noble Truths: (1) all living beings suffer; (2) the origin of this suffering is desired for material possessions, power, etc.; (3) desire can be overcome; and (4) there is a path that leads to release from desire. This way is called the Noble Eightfold Path:

1. **Right View** – The right way to think about life is to see the world through the eyes of the Buddha – with wisdom and compassion.
2. **Right Thought** – We are what we think. Clear and kind thoughts build good, strong characters.
3. **Right Speech** – By speaking kind and helpful words, we are respected and trusted by everyone.
4. **Right Conduct** – No matter what we say, others know us from the way we behave. Before we criticize others, we should first see what we do ourselves.
5. **Right Livelihood** – This means choosing a job that does not hurt others. The Buddha said, "Do not earn your living by harming others. Do not seek happiness by making others unhappy."
6. **Right Effort** – A worthwhile life means doing our best at all times and having good will toward others. This also means not wasting effort on things that harm ourselves and others.
7. **Right Mindfulness** – This means being aware of

our thoughts, words, and deeds.

8. **Right Concentration** – Focus on one thought or object at a time. By doing this, we can be quiet and attain true peace of mind.

Gautama promoted the concept of anatman (that a person has no actual self) and the idea that existence is characterized by impermanence. This realization helps one let go of desire for transient things. Still, Gautama did not recommend extreme self-denial but rather a disciplined life called the Middle Way. Like the Hindus, he believed that existence consisted of reincarnation, a cycle of birth and death. He held that it could be broken only by reaching complete detachment from worldly cares. Then the soul can be released into nirvana (literally "blowing out") an indescribable state of total transcendence. Gautama traveled to preach the dharma (sacred truth) and was recognized as the Buddha (enlightened one). After his death his followers continued to develop doctrine and practice, which came to center on the Three Jewels: the dharma (the sacred teachings of Buddhism); the sangha (the community of followers, which now includes nuns, monks and laity), and the Buddha. Under the patronage of the Mauryan emperor Ashoka (third century B.C.), Buddhism spread throughout India and to other parts of Asia. Monasteries were established, as well as temples dedicated to Buddha; at shrines his relics were venerated. Though by the fourth century A.D. Buddhist presence in India had dwindled, it flourished in other parts of Asia. Between the second century B.C. and the second century A.D., the Mahayana (Greater Vehicle) tradition refocused Buddhism to concentrate less on individual attainment of enlightenment and more on concern for humanity. It promotes the ideal of the bodhisattva (enlightened being), who shuns entering nirvana until all sentient beings can do so as well, willingly remaining in the painful cycle of birth and death to perform works of compassion. Members of this tradition conceive of Buddha as an eternal being to whom prayers can be made; other Buddhas are revered as well, adding a polytheistic dimension to the religion. Numerous sects have developed from the Mahayana tradition, which has been influential in China, Korea and Japan. All religions have some basic rules that define what is good conduct and what should be avoided. In Buddhism, the most important rules are the Five Precepts, which were passed down from the Buddha himself:

1. **No killing** – The Buddha said, "Life is dear to all beings. They have the right to live the same as we do." We should respect all life and not kill anything. Killing ants and mosquitoes is also breaking this precept. We should have an attitude of loving-kindness toward all things, wishing them to be happy and free from harm. Taking care of the earth, its rivers and air is included. One way that Buddhists follow this precept is by being vegetarian.

2. **No stealing** – If we steal from another, we steal from ourselves. Instead, we should learn to give and take care of things that belong to our family, to the school or to the public.

3. **No sexual misconduct** – Proper conduct shows respect for oneself and others. Our bodies are gifts from our parents, so we should protect them from harm. Young people should especially keep their natures pure and develop their virtue. It is up to them to make the world a better place to live. In happy families, the husband and wife both respect each other.

4. **No lying** – Being honest brings peace into the world. When there is a misunderstanding, the best thing is to talk it over. This precept includes no gossip, no backbiting, no harsh words and no idle speech.

5. **No intoxicants** – This precept is based on keeping a

clear mind and a healthy body. The worst thing is to lose your wisdom and become stupid.

Christianity – is a monotheistic religion founded by the followers of Jesus of Nazareth. The word Christianity derives from the Latin word "Christ," which is a translation of the Hebrew word Meshiyach (in English, "messiah"). In its original Hebrew expression, Christ means "Anointed" or "Anointed One." The word Christianity does not appear anywhere in the Bible. The word Christian or Christians is mentioned in only three places (Acts 11:24; 26:28; 1 Peter 4: 16). Jesus was not a Christian; he was a Jew, his parents, disciples and followers were Jews. Jesus was born in about 7 B.C. and assumed his public life, probably after his 30th year, in Galilee. The New Testament Gospels describe Jesus as a teacher and miracle worker. He proclaimed the kingdom of God, a future reality that is at the same time already present. Jesus set the requirements for participation in the Kingdom of God as a change of heart and repentance for sins, love of God and neighbor and concern for justice. Circa A.D. 30 he was executed on a cross in Jerusalem, a brutal form of punishment for those considered a political threat to the Roman Empire. After his death his followers came to believe in him as the Christ, the Messiah. The Gospels report his resurrection and how the risen Jesus was witnessed by many of his followers. The apostle Paul helped spread the new faith in his missionary travels. Historically, Christianity arose out of Judaism and claims that Jesus fulfilled many of the promises of the Hebrew Scripture (often referred to as the Old Testament). The new religion spread rapidly throughout the Roman Empire. In its first two centuries, Christianity began to take shape as an organization, developing distinctive doctrine, liturgy and ministry. By the fourth century the Christian church had taken root in countries stretching from Spain in the West to Persia and India in the East. The differences in doctrine threatened to divide the church, a standard Christian creed formulated by bishops at successive ecumenical councils, the first of which was held in A.D. 325 (Nicaea). Important doctrines were defined concerning the Trinity such as, there is one God in three persons: Father, Son and Holy Spirit (Constantinople, A.D. 381) and the nature of Christ as both divine and human (Chalcedon, A.D. 541). Christians came to accept both Hebrew Scripture and the New Testament as authoritative, however due to the differences between Christians of the East and West, the unity of the church was broken in 1054. In 1517 the Reformation began, which ultimately caused a schism in the Western church. Reformers wished to correct certain practices within the Roman church, but they also came to view the Christian faith in a distinctly new way. In the 21st century, many Christians hoped to regain a sense of unity through dialogue and cooperation among different traditions. The ecumenical movement led to the formation of the World Council of Churches in 1948 (Amsterdam), which has since been joined by many denominations. The sources of the Christian faith are the Holy Bible with the Old and New Testaments. There are a number of versions to the Bible with the King James Version possibly the widely used; it has scriptures (66 books), chapters within the books and host of verses within the chapters. The following are the eight primary versions of Bibles found in history:

1. Septuagint – 250 C.E. Written in Greek
2. Vulgate – 400 C.E. First version of the Bible which is canonized of Carthage in 400 C.E. Written in Latin
3. Luther's German Bible – 1524 C.E.
4. King James Version – 1611 C.E. This is the most widely used version however it has large number of errors given that none of the writers had a decent understanding of Hebrew.
5. Revised Standard Version – 1952 C.E. Liberal translation into American English which used the earliest

possible text

6. New International Version – 1960's & 70's C.E. This is a conservative, contemporary English version
7. Jerusalem Bible – 1966 C.E. This is the first version of the Bible to be commissioned by the Catholic Church since the 400's.
8. New Revised Standard Version – 1990 C.E. this is the most academic and scholarly version with the most accurately possible translations of the original text.

Confucianism – Confucius (K'ung Fu-tzu), born in the state of Lu (northern China), lived from 551 to 479 B.C. He was a brilliant teacher, viewing education not merely as the accumulation of knowledge but as a means of self-transformation. His legacy was a system of thought emphasizing education, proper behavior and loyalty. His effect on Chinese culture was immense; his teachings are contained in the Analects, a collection of his sayings as remembered by his students. His teachings were developed greatly by philosophers such as Mencius (Meng Tse, fl. 400 B.C.). Confucianism is little concerned with metaphysical discussion of religion or with spiritual attainments; it emphasizes moral conduct and right relationships in the human sphere. Cultivation of virtue is a central tenet of Confucianism. Two important virtues are jen, a benevolent and humanitarian attitude and li, maintaining proper relationship and rituals that enhance the life of the individuals, the family and the state. The "five relations," between king and subject, father and son, man and wife, older and younger brother, and friend and friend, are of utmost importance. These relationships are reinforced by participation in rituals, including the formal procedures of court life and religions such as ancestor worship. Confucius revolutionized educational thought in China, which he believed learning was not to be focused only on attaining the skills for a particular profession, but for growth in moral judgment and self-realization. Confucius's standards for the proper conduct of government shaped the statecraft of China for centuries. Hundreds of temples in honor of Confucius testify to his stature as sage and teacher. Confucianism was far less dominant in 20th-century China, at least on an official level. The state cult of Confucius was ended in 1911, however his traditions and moral standards are part of the cultural essence of China and other East Asian countries.

Hinduism – is the major religion of India, practiced by more than 80% of the population. In contrast to other religions, it has no founder, but is considered the oldest religion in the world; it dates back to prehistoric times. No single creed or doctrine binds Hindus together, intellectually there is complete freedom of belief and individual can be monotheist, polytheist or atheist. Hinduism is a syncretism religion, welcoming and incorporating a variety of outside influences. The most important texts of the Hindu religion are written in Sanskrit and called the Vedas (Vedas means "knowledge"). There are four Vedic books, of which the Rig-Veda is the oldest. It discusses multiples gods, the universe and creation. The dates of these works are unknown (1000 B.C.?). Present-day Hindus rarely refer to these texts but do venerate them. The Upanishads (dated 1000 – 300 B.C.), commentaries on the Vedic texts, speculate on the origin of the universe and the nature of deity, and atman (the individual soul) and its relationship to Brahman (the universal soul). They introduce the doctrine of karma and recommend meditation and the practice of yoga. Other important sacred writings include the Epics, which contains legendary stories about gods and humans. They are the Mahabharata (composed between 200 B.C. and A.D. 200) and the Ramayana. The former includes the Bhagavad-Gita (Song of the Lord), and influential text that describes the three paths to salvation. The Puranas (stories in verse, probably written between the 6th and 13th centuries) detail myths of Hindu gods and heroes and also comment on religious practice and cosmology. According to Hindu beliefs, Brahman is the principle and source of the universe. This divine intelligence pervades all beings, including the individual soul. Thus the many Hindu deities are manifestations of the one Brahman. Hinduism is based on the concept of reincarnation, in which all living beings, from plants on earth to gods above, are caught in a cosmic cycle of becoming and perishing. The law of karma determines life; an individual is born to a higher level of existence based on moral behavior in a previous phase of existence. Life on earth is regarded as transient and a burden. The goal of existence is liberation from the cycle of rebirth and death and entrance into indescribable state of moksha (liberation). The practice of Hinduism consists of rites and ceremonies centering on birth, marriage and death. There are many Hindu temples, which are considered to be dwelling places of the deities and to which people bring offerings. Places of pilgrimage include Benares on the Ganges, the most sacred river in India. Of the many Hindu deities, the most popular are the cults of Vishnu, Shiva and Shakti, and their various incarnations. Also important is Brahma, the creator god. Hindus also venerate human saints. Orthodox Hindu society in India was divided into four major hereditary classes: (1) the Brahmin (priestly and learned class); (2) the Kshatriya (military, professional, ruling and governing occupations); (3) the Vaishya (landowners, merchants and business occupations); and (4) the Sudra (artisans, laborers and peasants). Below the Sudra was a fifth group, the Untouchables (lowest menial occupations and no social standing). The Indian government banned discrimination against the Untouchables in the constitution of India in 1950. Observance of class and caste distinctions varies throughout India. In modern times work has been done to reform and revive Hinduism. One of the outstanding reformers was Ramakrishna (1836 – 1886), who inspired many followers, one of whom founded the Ramakrishna mission.

Islam – Muhammad founded Islam, one of the three major monotheistic faiths, in Arabia between 610 and 632. There are an estimated 5.1 million Muslims in North America and 1.3 billion Muslims worldwide. Muhammad was born in A.D. 570 at Mecca and belonged to the Quraysh tribe, which was active in the caravan trade. At the age of 25 he joined the trade from Mecca to Syria in the employment of a rich widow, Khadija, whom he later married. Critical of the lax moral standards and polytheistic practices of the inhabitants of Mecca, he began to lead a contemplative life in the desert. In a dramatic religious vision, the angel Gabriel announced to Muhammad that he was to be a prophet. Khadija, his wife, encouraged him, so he devoted himself to reforming religion, society and abandoned polytheism. However, the leaders of Quraysh tribe generally rejected his teaching, which resulted in Muhammad gaining only a small following and suffered persecution, so he eventually fled Mecca. Muhammad moved (Hijra, meaning "emigration) from Mecca, where he was not honored, to Medina where he was well received; this occurred in 622 and marked the beginning of the Muslim era (Muslim, meaning "members of Islam religion"). After a number of military conflicts with Mecca, he marched on Mecca in 630 and conquered it. Muhammad died at Medina in 632; his grave has since been a place of pilgrimage. Muhammad's followers, called Muslims, revered him as the prophet of Allah (God), the only God. Muslims consider Muhammad to be the last in the line of prophets that included Abraham and Jesus. The Islamic religion spread quickly from Spain in the west to India in the east within a century after Muhammad's death. Sources of the Islamic faith are the Qur'an (Koran), which is comprised of 114 Surahs (chapters) and 6236 Ayats (verses) regarded as the uncreated, eternal Word of God and tradition (hadith) sayings and deeds of Muhammad. Islam means "surrender to the will of Allah," the all-powerful, who determines humanity's fate, while good deeds will be rewarded at the last judgment in paradise and evil deeds will be punished in hell. The Five Pillars, or primary duties, of Islam are (1) testimony of faith; (2) prayer, to be performed five times a day; (3)

almsgiving to the poor and the mosque (house of worship); (4) fasting during daylight hours in the month of Ramadan; and (5) pilgrimage to Mecca (the hajj) at least once in a Muslim's lifetime, if it is physically and financially possible. The pilgrimage includes homage to the ancient shrine of the Ka'aba, the most sacred site in Islam. On Fridays, Muslims gather for corporate worship, prayers and a sermon take place at the mosque, which is also a center for teaching of the Qur'an. The imam is considered a teacher and prayer leader. Islam succeeded in uniting an Arab world of separate tribes and castes, but disagreements concerning the succession of Muhammad caused a division in Islam between two groups, Sunnis and Shi'ites. The Shi'ites rejected the first three successors to Muhammad as usurpers, claiming the fourth, Muhammad's son-in-law Ali, as the rightful leader. The Sunnis (from the word tradition), the largest division of Islam (today more than 80%), believe in the legitimacy of the first three successors. Other sects arose (such as the conservative Wahhabi of Saudi Arabia) as well as different schools of theology. Another development within Islam, beginning in the eighth and ninth centuries, was Sufism, a form of mysticism, this movement was influential for many centuries and was instrumental in the spread of Islam in Asia and Africa. Islam has expanded greatly under Muhammad's successors; it is the principal religion of the Middle East, Asia and the northern half of Africa.

Jainism – differs from other religion in its concept of a god. Jainism regards every living soul as potentially divine. When the soul sheds its karmic bonds completely, it attains God-consciousness. It prescribes a path of nonviolence to progress the soul to this ultimate goal. A Jain is a follower of Jinas ("conquerors"), who are spiritually advanced human beings who rediscover the dharma, become fully liberated and teach the spiritual path to benefit all living beings. Practicing Jains follow the teachings of 24 special jinas who are known as Tirthankaras ("ford-makers," or "those who have discovered and shown the way to salvation"). Tradition states that the 24th and most recent, Tirthankar is Shri Mahavir, lived from 599 to 527 B.C. The 23rd Tirthankar, Shri Parsva, lived from 872 to 772 B.C. Jainism encourages spiritual development through reliance on and cultivation of one's own personal wisdom and self-control (vrata). The goal of Jainism is to realize the soul's true nature. "Samyak darshan gyan charitrani moksha margah," meaning "true/right perception, knowledge and conduct" (known as the triple gems of Jainism) provides the path for attaining liberation (moksha) from samsara (the universal cycle of birth and death). Moksha is attained by liberation from karma. Those who have attained moksha are called siddha (liberated souls), and those who are attached to the world through their karma are called samsarin (mundane souls). Every soul has to follow the path, as described by the Jinas (and revived by Tirthankaras), to attain the ultimate liberation. The literal meaning of Tirthankar is "ford-builder." Jains, like Buddhists, compare the process of becoming a pure human to crossing a swift river, an endeavor requiring patience and care. A ford-builder has already crossed the river and can therefore guide others. Like Buddhism, the purpose of Jain dharma is to undo the negative effects of karma through mental and physical purification. This process leads to liberation accompanied by a great natural inner peace. Having purified one's soul of karmic impurities, a tirthankar is considered omniscient and a role model. Jains believe that every human is responsible for his/her actions and all living beings have an eternal soul, jiva. Further, Jains believe all souls are equal because they all possess the potential of being liberated and attaining moksha. Jains insist that we live, think and act respectfully and honor the spiritual nature of all life. Jains view God as the unchanging traits of the pure soul of each living being, described as Infinite Knowledge, Perception, Consciousness and Happiness (Ananta Jnana, Ananta Darshana, Ananta Caritra and Ananta Sukha). Jains do not believe in an omnipotent supreme being, creator or manager (karta), rather in an eternal universe governed by natural laws. The ethical code of Jainism is taken very seriously, which is summarized in the following Five Vows; they are adhered to both lay people and monastics, which are:

1. Nonviolence (ahinsa or ahimsa)
2. Truth (satya)
3. Non-stealing (asteya)
4. Chastity (brahmacharya)
5. Non-possession or non-possessiveness (aparigrah)

Judaism – is the oldest of the monotheistic faiths, it affirms the existence of one God, Yahweh, who entered into covenant with the descendants of Abraham, God's chosen people. Judaism's holy writings reveal how God has been present with them throughout their history. These writings are known as the Torah (their central religious text), specifically the five books of Moses, but most broadly conceived as the Hebrew Scriptures (traditionally called the Old Testament by Christians) and the compilation of oral tradition known as the Talmud (which includes the Mishnah, the oral law). According to Scripture, the Hebrew patriarch Abraham (20th century B.C.) founded the faith that would become known as Judaism. He obeyed the call of God to depart northern Mesopotamia and travel to Canaan. God promised to bless his descendants if they remained faithful in worship. Abraham's line descended through Isaac, then Jacob (also called Israel; his descendants came to be called Israelites). Accordingly to Scripture, 12 families that descended from Jacob migrated to Egypt, where they were enslaved. They were led out of bondage by Moses, who united them in worship of Yahweh (13th century B.C.). The Hebrews returned to Canaan after a 40-year sojourn in the desert, conquering from the local peoples the "promised land" that God had provided for them. The 12 tribes of Israel lived in a covenant during the period of the judges (1200? – 1005? B.C.); his successor, David (r. 1005? – 965? B.C.), unified the land of Israel and made Jerusalem its religious and political center. Under his son, Solomon (r. 968? – 928? B.C.), a golden era culminated in the building of a temple, replacing the portable sanctuary in use until that time. Following Solomon's death, the Kingdom was split into Israel in the north and Judah in the south. However, political conflicts resulted in the conquest of Israel by Assyria (721 B.C.) and the defeat of Judah by Babylon (586 B.C.). Jerusalem and its temple were destroyed and many Judeans were exiled to Babylon. Moving forward, after a respite during the 18th-century Enlightenment, anti-Semitism again plagued European Jews in the 19th century, sparking the Zionist movement that culminated in the founding of the state of Israel in 1948. The Holocaust of World War II took the lives of more than 6 million Jews. However, Jews today continue synagogue worship, which includes readings from the Law and the Prophets and prayers, such as the Shema (Hear, O Israel) and the Amidah (the 18 Benedictions). Religious life is guided by the commandments of Torah, which include the practice of circumcision and Sabbath observance. Present-day Judaism has three main expressions: Orthodox, Conservative and Reform. Reform movements, resulting from the Haskala (Jewish Enlightenment) of the 18th century, began in Western Europe but took root in North America. Reform Jews do not hold the oral law (Talmud) to be a divine revelation and they emphasize ethical and moral teachings. Orthodox Jews follow the traditional faith and practice with great seriousness; they follow a strict kosher diet and observe the Sabbath with care. Conservative Judaism, which developed in the mid-18th century, holds the Talmud to be authoritative and follows most traditional practices, yet tries to make Judaism relevant for each generation, believing that change and tradition can complement each other. A Jewish identity is not dependent upon accepting the Torah; a strong secular movement also exists within Jewish life, including atheist and agnostic elements. In general, Jews do not proselytize, but they do welcome newcomers to their faith.

Shinto – comprises the religious ideas and practices indigenous to Japan. Ancient Shinto focused on the worship of the kami, a host of supernatural beings that could be known through forms (objects of nature, remarkable people, abstract concepts such as justice) but were ultimately mysterious. Shinto has no formal dogma and no holy writ, though early collections of Japanese religious thought and practice (kojiki, "Records of Ancient Matters," A.D. 712 and Nihon shoki, "Chronicles of Japan," A.D. 720) are highly regarded. Shinto has been influenced by Confucianism and by Buddhism, which was introduced in Japan in the 6th century. Syncretic schools (such as Ryobu Shinto) emerged, as did other sects that rejected Buddhism (such as Ise Shinto). Under the reign of the emperor Meiji (1868 – 1912), Shinto became the official state religion. State Shinto, the national cult, emphasized the divinity of the emperor, whose succession was traced back to the first emperor, Jimmu (660 B.C.), and beyond him to the sun goddess Amaterasu-o-mi-kami. State Shinto was disestablished after World War II. Sect Shinto, deriving from sects that developed during the 19th and 20th centuries, continues to thrive in Japan. Shrines dedicated to particular kami are visited by parishioners for prayer and traditional ceremonies, such as presenting a newborn child to the kami. Tradition festivals celebrated at the shrines include purification rites, presentation of food offerings, prayer, sacred music and dance, and a feast. No particular day of the week is set-aside for prayer; a person may visit a shrine at will, entering through the torii (gateway). It is believed that the kami can respond to prayer and can offer protection and guidance. A variety of Shinto sects and practices exist today. Ten-rikyo emphasizes faith healing. Folk Shinto is characterized by veneration of roadside shrines and rites related to agriculture. Buddhist priests serve at many Shinto shrines and many families keep a small shrine, or god-shelf, at home. Veneration of ancestors and pilgrimage are also common practices. Shinto is not defined by a vast array of doctrinal ideas. A fundamental goal or aim of Shinto is the attainment of makoto no kokoro (□□□ "true heart," "sincerity"). When one has "true heart," he/she is open to the subtle movements and presence of the spiritual forces known as kami. Shinto belief and practice have traditionally been threefold:

- It is indigenous, in that it expresses reverence for the land of Japan.
- It is animistic, in that it expresses reverence for nature.
- It is spiritualistic, in that it expresses reverence for ancestors.

Sikhism – A major religion of India and the fifth-largest faith in the world, Sikhism emerged in the Punjab under the guidance of the guru Nanak (1469 – 1539?). This region had been influenced by the Hindu bhakti movement, which promoted both the idea that God comprises one reality alone as well as the practice of devotional singing and prayer. The Muslim mystical tradition of Sufism, with its emphasis on meditation, also had some prominence there. Drawing on these resources, Nanak forged a new spiritual path. In his youth, Nanak began to compose hymns, at age 29, he had a mystical experience that led him to proclaim, "There is no Hindu and there is no Muslim." A strict monotheist, he rejected Hindu polytheism but accepted the Hindu concept of life as a cycle of birth, death and rebirth; moksha, released from this cycle into unity with God, could be achieved only with the help of a guru or spiritual teacher. Nanak believed that communion with God could be gained through devotional repetition of the divine name, singing of hymns and praises and adherence to a demanding ethical code. He rejected idols and the Hindu caste system; it became a custom for Sikhs of all social ranks to take meals together, these beliefs are still central to modern Sikhism. Nanak was first in a line of ten gurus who shaped Sikhism. The fifth, Arjun (1563 – 1606), compiled hymns and other writings by earlier Sikh gurus, as well as medieval Hindu and Muslim saints, in the Adi Granth (First Book), or Guru Granth Sahib (the Granth Personified). This book became the sacred scripture of Sikhism. In addition to his spiritual leadership, Arjun wielded considerable secular power as he grappled with leaders of the Mughal Empire. The tenth guru, Gobind Singh (1666 – 1708), was both a scholar and a military hero, he established the Khalsa (community of pure ones), an order that combined spiritual devotion, personal discipline and ideals of military valor. Baptism initiates new members into the Khalsa. The Adi Granth took its final form under the supervision of Gobind Singh, as did the Dasam Granth (Tenth Book), a collection of prayers, poetry and narrative. After the deaths of his four sons, Gobind Singh declared the line of gurus at an end. The Adi Granth would instead be reverenced in houses of worship, taking the place of a living guru. Today, Sikhs worship at gurdwaras (temples), where the Adi Granth is the object of devotion. This book is consulted regarding questions of faith and practice, on certain occasions, it is recited in its entirety (requiring more than a day) or carried in procession; offering may be placed before it. Worshipful singing, meditation and focus on the divine name remain essential to spiritual life. Some Sikhs undertake pilgrimages to historical gurdwaras, such as the Golden Temple of Amritsar, that are associated with the guru; some become disciples of living saints. There is no established Sikh priesthood. Sikh beliefs are:

- **Goal**: The goal of Sikhs is to build a close, loving relationship with God.
- **Deity:** Sikhs believe in a single, formless God, with many names, who can be known through meditation. His concept is similar to Islam whose followers believe in a single God, who has 99 names. Daily many Sikhs recite the Mool Mantar, the first hymn composed by Guru Nanak. It contains a description of many of the attributes of God: There is only one God, his name is Truth; He is the Creator; He is without fear; He is without hate; He is beyond time (i.e. is immortal); He is beyond birth and death; He is self-existent. Only he can be worshiped. Rahras, a Sikh evening prayer states; "[O God] since I

have fallen at your feet, I do not care for anybody else. I do not follow the religious ways preached by various religions believing in Ram, Mohammed, Puran or Qur'an. The Simritis, Shastras and the Vedas lay down different doctrines. But I do not recognize any of these. O God, I have written these hymns with your grace and kindness. All that has been said is in fact spoken by you."

- **Reincarnation:** They believe in samsara (the repetitive cycle of birth, life and death), karma (the accumulated sum of one's good and bad deeds, and reincarnation the belief of a rebirth following death). These beliefs are similar to Hinduism. "Each individual has many reincarnations, but being born a human means the soul is nearing the end of rebirth. God judges each soul at death and may either reincarnate the soul or, if pure enough, allow it to rest with him."

- **Caste system:** Sikhs have rejected the caste system of the Hindu religion. They believe that everyone has equal status in the eyes of God. This is a very important principle that permeates all Sikh beliefs, behaviors and rituals.

- **Code of Conduct:** During the 18th century, there were a number of attempts to prepare an accurate portrayal of Sikh customs. None received the support of most Sikhs. Sikhs scholars and theologians started in 1931 to prepare the Reht Maryada – the Sikh code of conduct and conventions. It is "the only version authorized by the Akal Takht, the seat of supreme temporal authority for Sikhs. Its implementation has successfully achieved a high level of uniformity in the religious and social practices of Sikhism" throughout the world. Sikh practices are:

- **Prayers:** repeated multiple times each day.

- **Worship:** Sikhs are prohibited from worshipping idols,

images or icons.

- **Temples:** there are over 200 Gurdwaras (temples, shrines or holy places) in India alone. The most sacred is Harmandir Sahib, the Golden Temple, at Amritsar. However, all places where the Sri Guru Granth Sahib is installed are equally holy.
- **The Five K's:** These are clothing practices followed by stricter Sikhs, called khalsa saints;
    1. Kesa (long hair, which is never cut). This term is sometimes used to refer to the turban that is used to cover the hair.
    2. Kangah (comb)
    3. Kacha (short pants)
    4. Kara (metal bracelet)
    5. Kirpan (a ceremonial dagger)
- Drinking of alcoholic beverages is forbidden.
- Smoking is forbidden.

Taoism – is one of the major religions of China based on ancient philosophical works, primarily the Tao Te Ching, "Classic of Tao and its Virtue." Traditionally, this book was thought to be the work of Lao-tzu, a quasi-historical philosopher of the 6th century B.C.; scholars now believe that the book dates from about the 3rd century B.C. The philosopher Chuang Tzu (4th – 3rd centuries B.C.) also contributed to the seminal ideas of Taoism. Toa, "the Way," is the ultimate reality of the universe, according to Taoism, it is a creative process and humans can live in harmony with it by clearing themselves of obstacles. By cultivating wu-wei, a type of inaction characterized by humility and prudence, a person can participate in the simplicity and spontaneity of Tao. Striving to attain virtue or achievement is counterproductive and unnecessary. Taoism values mystical contemplation and balance. The human being is viewed as a microcosm of the universe and the Chinese principle of yin-yang, complementary duality, is a model of harmony. The religious practices of Taoism emerged from these ancient philosophies and from Chinese shamanistic tradition; by the 2nd century A.D., it constituted an organized religion. Longevity and immortality were sought through regulating the energies of the body through breathing exercises, meditation and use of medicinal plants, talismans and magical formulas. A cult of immortals, including the divined Lao-tzu, also developed. Influenced by Buddhism, Taoists organized monastic orders. Temple worship and forms of divination, including the I ching, were practiced. Since it beginnings, many sects have arisen within Taoism, all subscribe to the philosopher origins of the region; some have emphasized faith healing, exorcism, the worship of the immortals, meditation or alchemy. Buddhism and Confucianism influenced some sects, others operated as secret societies. Though the present Chinese government has tried to suppress it, Taoism is still practiced in mainland China, Taiwan and Hong Kong. It profoundly influenced Chinese art and literature and Taoist ideas have become popular in the West. The following are Taoist concepts beliefs and practices:

- Tao is the first-cause of the universe; it is a force that flows through all life.
- "The Tao surrounds everyone and therefore everyone must listen to find enlightenment."
- Each believer's goal is to harmonize himself or herself with the Tao.
- Taoism has provided an alternative to the Confucian tradition in China. The two traditions have coexisted in the country, region and generally within the same individual.
- The priesthood views the many gods as manifestations of the one Dao, "which could not be represented as an image or a particular thing." The con-

cept of a personal deity is foreign to them, as is the concept of the creation of the universe. Thus, they do not pray as Christians do; there is no God to pray to or act upon them. They seek answers to life's problems through inner meditation and outer observation.

- In contrast with the beliefs and practices of the priesthood, most of the laity has "believed that spirits pervaded nature…The gods in heaven acted like and were treated like the officials in the world of men; worshipping the gods were the kind of rehearsal of attitudes toward secular authorities. On the other hand, the demons and ghosts of hell acted like and were treated like the bullies, outlaws and threatening strangers in the real world; they were bribed by the people and were ritually arrested by the marital forces of the officials."
- Time is cyclical, not linear as in Western thinking.
- Taoists strongly promote health and vitality.
- Five main organs and offices of the body correspond to the five parts of the sky: water, fire, wood, mental and earth.
- Each person must nurture the Ch'i (air, breath) that has been given to him or her.
- Development of virtue is one's chief task. The Three Jewels to be sought are: compassion, moderation and humility.
- Taoist follow the art of "wu wei," which is to let nature take it course. For example, one should allow a river to flow towards the sea unimpeded; do not erect a dam, which would interfere with its natural flow.

- One should plan in advance and consider carefully each action before making it.
- A Taoists is kind to other individuals, in part because such an action tends to be reciprocated.
- Taoists believe that "people are compassionate by nature...left to their own devices [they] will show this compassion without expecting a reward."

Zoroastrianism: - believes that the world is a combination both good and evil; creation cannot exist without the presence of both. In the beginning of creation, Ahura Mazda, the Supreme God, created two Mainyus or twin spirits called Spenta Mainyu, the good spirit and Angra Mainyu (Ahirman), the evil spirit. Creation is possible only when they both come together. Spenta Mainyu is responsible for all the good works in the creation of God. He exists in all of us and helps us to see the light within ourselves. Ahirman is an illusion, he exists in order to make us understand that true existence means. By opposing good, he makes us realize the importance and necessity of good in our lives. In this eternal conflict Ahirman ultimately loses out to Spenta Mainyu. It is to be noted that neither Ahirman nor Spenta Mainyu are absolute powers. They are the creation of God and work according to His Divine Plan, or Asha. According to Zoroastrian doctrine, Ahura Mazda is a perfect, rational and omniscient (all-knowing) entity. Thus, Zoroastrians believe that Angra Mainyu created sin, disease, death and similar evils. Ahura Mazda is said to have created six Amesha Spentas ("Holy Immortals"), who represent aspects of material creation, in addition to other minor spiritual beings who assisted in protecting the world and all creatures. Angra Mainyu is said to have produced numerous Daevas (demonic spirits), who represents aspects of pain, suffering and death, to attack Ahura Mazda's creations. Many of the spirits worshiped or renounced by Zoroastrians also appear in early Hindu texts because the ancient Iranians and Indians shared a religious and linguistic heritage. Zoroastrians believe that Ahura Mazda created humans as allies in the cosmic struggle against evil and that humanity will be resurrected and granted immortality once evil has been defeated. They further view the material world as a trap into which evil has been lured and in which evil will undergo defeat by divinities and humans working together. Zoroastrianism preaches that when someone dies his or her soul undergoes individual judgment based on actions while alive. If the soul's good deeds are greater than its evil deeds, it enters paradise. If the soul's evil deeds outweigh the good done while alive, it is cast into hell to wait the day of universal judgment. In cases where a soul's good deeds equal its evil deeds, it is consigned to limbo. Zoroastrianism claims, close to the end of time a savior will resurrect the dead and Ahura Mazda will descend to earth with the other good spirits. Each sinner, having already suffered in hell or limbo after death, will be purified. Thereafter, immortality will be granted to all humans. Ahura Mazda, the holy immortals and other divine beings will annihilate the demons and force Angra Mainyu to shuttle back into hell, which will then be sealed. The Zoroastrian doctrine of heaven, hell, and limbo influenced other faiths. Islam absorbed not only the ideas of heaven, hell and limbo, but also the scheme of individual judgment at a celestial bridge and the notion of final, universal judgment. Christianity further assimilated the Zoroastrian belief of the soul's afterlife and the appearance of a savior, resurrection and eternal life at the end of the world. Zoroastrianism, like other religions, possesses a tradition of sacred stories. Most important is the account of creation, preserved in the Bundahishn, or Book of Primal Creation. It tells of the first human, Gayo Maretan (also known as Gayomard or Kaymurs), who had both male and female characteristics, and of Gayo Maretan's descendants, the first human couple, Mashya and Mashyana. Apocalyptic and eschatological tales – that is, stories about the end of the world and salvation – are founding the Wizidagiha or Selections and other sources. These tales predict the defeat of evil, the resurrection, the making complete or renewal of the world (known as frasho-kereti or frashagird), and the final triumph and perpetual establishment of order and truth. Myths of spirits, such as Tishtrya (Tistar or Sirius) who presides over rain, are found in the yashts (hymns or devotional poems) of the Avesta and are popularly called towers of silence. Zoroastrians bury or cremate their deceased.

The above discussions are designed to provide valuable information regarding the world twelve major religions, in order to identify the similarities and differences among them. Also, it provides a comprehensive basis for further study of these world religions. Consequently, we can see in some cases the concepts, beliefs and practices that support one religious tradition is relevant in one or more other religions. Even though the names of the various religions, their sacred texts, places of worship and titles of their leaders are different; however one can find some similarities. Hopefully, this information will help lessen the religious debates on, **"my religion is better than yours."** We must know and accept that life is good. Life is the Almighty Divine Supreme Creator, who is not religious [we are], but the Creator permeates all religions and all that is good and perfect. The Creator does not reside in a church, a bible, a doctrine, a ritual or a sermon. The Almighty Divine Supreme Creator resides in you and me and every one of us. We are each a church, a temple, a mosque, a synagogue or any other similar holy place. Christ resides in each of us; we must find the wisdom, the knowledge and the understanding to know and accept it. George MacDonald said, "I suspect that worse dishonesty, and greater injustice, are to be found among the champions, lay and cleric, of religious opinion than in any other class." The following charts will provide some additional information on various religions:

Basic information on various religions:

Religion	Date Founded	Sacred Texts	Membership 5	% of World 6
Christianity	30 CE	The Bible	2,039 million	32% (dropping)
Islam	622 CE	Qur'an & Hadith	1,226 million	19% (growing)
Hinduism	1500 BCE with truly ancient roots	Bhagavad-Gita, Upanishads, & Rig Veda	828 million	13% (stable)
No religion (Note 1)	-	None	775 million	12% (dropping)
Chinese folk rel.	270 BCE	None	390 million	6%
Buddhism	523 BCE	The Tripitaka & Sutras	364 million	6% (stable)
Tribal Religions, Shamanism, Animism	Prehistory	Oral tradition	232 million	4%
Atheists	No date	None	150 million	2%
New religions.	Various	Various	103 million	2%
Sikhism	1500 CE	Guru Granth Sahib	23.8 million	<1%
Judaism	Note 3	Torah, Tanach, & Talmud	14.5 million	<1%
Spiritism			12.6 million	<1%

Baha'i Faith	1863 CE	Alkitab Alaqdas	7.4 million	<1%
Confucianism	520 BCE	Lun Yu	6.3 million	<1%
Jainism	570 BCE	Siddhanta, Pakrit	4.3 million	<1%
Zoroastrianism	600 to 6000 BCE	Avesta	2.7 million	<1%
Shinto	500 CE	Kojiki, Nohon Shoki	2.7 million	<1%
Taoism	550 BCE	Tao-te-Ching	2.7 million	<1%
Other	Various	Various	1.1 million	<1%
Wicca	800 BCE, 1940 CE	None	0.5 million?	<1%

Names of the places of worship and English titles by which local leaders are called:

Religion	Place of worship	Title of local leader
Christianity	Church, Cathedral, Temple, Mission	Pastor, priest, minister
Islam	Mosque	Imam
No religion *	None	None
Hinduism	Mandir, Mandira, Temple, and other names	Priest
Buddhism	Pagoda, Stupa, Temple	Monk
Atheists	None	None
New Asian religion	Various	Various
Tribal Religions, Animism	In nature	Shaman
Judaism	Synagogue	Rabbi
Sikhism	Gurdwaras	Granthi (professional reader)
Shamanists	In nature	Shaman
Confucianism	Temple, Shrine, Seowon	Unknown
Baha'i Faith	House of worship	Usually a lay leader
Jainism	Temple	Priest, Pandit

Shinto	Temple	Priest
Wicca	Circle, Grove	Priestess, Priest, Wiccan
Zoroastrianism	Atash Behram, Agiyari, Prayer rooms	Mobed, Dastur

The above charts can help to identify when a given religion was founded; its sacred texts; number of members; their place of worship and the title of their leaders. Throughout humankind, the sacred scriptures of all religions have proclaimed that humanity is one great family. This is a simple truth and is stated in every religion, in that most of the principles, concepts, practices and beliefs associated with religious thought is shared by every religion. For example: *The Golden Rule; Love Thy Neighbor; Honor Thy Father and Mother; Speak the Truth;* and *It is More Blessed to Give Than to Receive.* These precepts and many others are common to all religions and are very similarly expressed in each, see below:

The Golden Rule

Do unto others as you would have them do unto you, for this is the law and the prophets.

Christianity

What is hurtful to yourself do not to your fellow man. That is the whole of the Torah and the remainder is but commentary.

Judaism

Do unto all men as you would they should unto you, and reject for others what you would reject for yourself.

Islam

Hurt not others with that which pains yourself.

Buddhism

What you do not yourself desire, do not put before others.

Confucianism

Treat others, as thou wouldst thyself be treated.
Do nothing to thy neighbor, which hereafter
thou wouldst not have thy neighbor do to thee.

Hinduism

Treat others as thou wouldst be treated thyself.

Sikhism

A man should wander about treating all creatures as he himself would
be treated.

Jainism

Regard your neighbor's gain as your own gain; and regard your neighbor's loss as your own loss, even as though you were in their place.

Taoism

Ascribe not to any soul that which thou wouldst not have ascribed to
thee.

Baha'i

There Is One God

There is one God and Father of all, who is above all, and through all,
and in you all.

Christianity

The Lord is God in heaven above and on the earth beneath; there is no other.

Judaism

He is the one God hidden in all beings, all-pervading, the Self within all beings, watching over all worlds, dwelling in all beings, the witness, the perceiver.

Hinduism

There is but one God whose name is true. He is the creator, immortal, unborn, self-existent.

Sikhism

All this is God. God is all that is.

Sufism

He, in truth, hath throughout eternity been one in His Essence, one in His attributes, one in His works.

Baha'i

Moderation in All Things

He who possesses moderation is lasting and enduring.

Taoism

Commit no excess; do nothing injurious... pleasures should not be carried to excess.

Confucianism

He who avoids extreme in eating and fasting,
In sleep and waking, and in work and play,
He wins balance, peace, and joy.

Hinduism

Let your moderation be known unto all men.

Christianity

If a man oversteps the limits of moderation, he pollutes his body and mind.

Shintoism

Observe moderation in all you do, and if that is not possible, try to be near moderation.

Islam

Heaven Is Within

The kingdom of God cometh not with observation: neither shall they say, Lo here! or, lo there! For, behold, the kingdom of God is within you.

Christianity

What the undeveloped man seeks is outside; what the advanced man seeks is within himself.

Confucianism

If you think the law is outside yourself, you are embracing not the absolute law but some inferior teaching.

Buddhism

If human beings knew their own inner secrets, they would never look elsewhere seeking for happiness and peace.

Sufism

God bides hidden in the hearts of all.

Hinduism

God is in thy heart, yet thou searchest for Him in the wilderness.

Sikhism

The above clearly show that the world's major religions have similar aims. I personally believe that religions may have substantial differences of philosophical concepts, but that they all have the same potential objective, which is the betterment of humankind. All religions may ask their followers to seek different paths and/or ways toward being enlightened. But beneath the differences is a pool of universal truths that guides them to inner peace, and allows them to achieve spiritual oneness. In Jeffrey Moses' book titled, *Oneness: Great Principles Shared By All Religions*, he states that:

> The scriptures of nearly every religion proclaim that the religion's founder was inspired directly by God. The ancient Vedic sage – Manu, Vyasa, and Shankara, among others – have been revered by millions of Hindus as direct channels of God to mankind. The Buddhist scriptures proclaim Buddha as the enlightened knower of the ultimate reality. Abraham, Moses, and other founders of Judaism are described in the Old Testament of the Holy Bible as speaking directly with God. The New Testament declares Jesus to be the Son of God, speaking, teaching, and acting as the channel for God's infinite wisdom. And Muslims have worshiped Mohammed, the founder of Islam, through the

centuries as the Prophet through whom Allah revealed the Holy Qur'an.

I am compelled to share with you that over 3500 years of recorded history before the advent of any of the above-mentioned religions existed; the Pagan Egyptians lived by a moral and ethical code called, *The 42 Principles of MA'AT* that has never been surpassed. However, as you read the aforementioned religions' beliefs, practices, commandments and/or principles, you will find some parts of the Ma'at's 42 moral codes. Ma'at was the Ancient Egyptian divine principle of *Truth, Justice and Righteousness,* which was the foundation of natural, social order and unity. Ma'at was the female counterpart to Tehurti and was the code for the living and the standard that the dead would be judged by. Egyptologists have termed the Ma'at principles as "Negative Confessions" because, they usually begin with the negative, "I have not." In the Ma'at principles of *Truth, Justice and Righteousness,* they are in fact affirmations of what one has not done in his or her life to live by Ma'at. *The 42 Principles Of Ma'at* are as follows:

1. I have not committed sin.
2. I have not committed robbery with violence.
3. I have not stolen.
4. I have not slain men and women.
5. I have not stolen food.
6. I have not swindled offerings.
7. I have not stolen from God.
8. I have not told lies.
9. I have not carried away food.
10. I have not cursed.
11. I have not committed fornication.
12. I have not committed adultery.
13. I have not made anyone cry.
14. I have not felt sorrow without reason.

15. I have not assaulted anyone.
16. I have not dealt deceitfully.
17. I have not stolen anyone's land.
18. I have not been an eavesdropper.
19. I have not falsely accused anyone.
20. I have not been angry without reason.
21. I have not seduced anyone's wife.
22. I have not polluted myself.
23. I have not terrorized anyone.
24. I have not disobeyed the law.
25. I have not been excessively angry.
26. I have not cursed God.
27. I have not behaved with violence.
28. I have not caused disruption of peace.
29. I have not acted hastily or without thought.
30. I have not overstepped my boundaries of concern.
31. I have not exaggerated my words when speaking.
32. I have not worked evil.
33. I have not used evil thoughts, words or deeds.
34. I have not polluted the water.
35. I have not spoken angrily or arrogantly.
36. I have not cursed anyone in thoughts, words or deeds.
37. I have not placed myself on a pedestal.
38. I have not stolen that which belongs to God.
39. I have not stolen from or disrespected the dead.
40. I have not taken food from a child.
41. I have not acted with insolence.
42. I have not destroyed property belonging to God.

It would be a wonderful world if we were to adopt *The 42 Principles of Ma'at* to guide us through our life experiences and pass them down to generations to come. Starting today, we should adopt these principles as a practical guide to moral and spiritual excellence to uplift humankind. I am reminded of the Teaching of Ptah-hotep written in 2370 B.C. that said, "Let your life be an example and live justly, for if justice remains a firm foundation, your children will prosper."

In summation, we can readily see that these holy teachers devoted their lives to guiding humanity toward the paths of righteousness. Even though their messages suited the vital necessities of their times; the inner truths of their teachings is quite relevant today. Thusly, we must see through our inner vision the Divinity in every person, every animal, every tree, as well as to appreciate their beauty. If we were to achieve this level of understanding and realization, *oh wow*, how different would our thinking be toward our existence? If we chose not, our lives will become consumed by this ill-nature mission; our marriages will suffer; our children well be neglected; our lives will wither in self-doubt and we might just self- destruct. We should all be known by our deeds, not by our religion. I will end as I started this discussion on "religion," by saying there is still a raging debate on the subject that goes on and on; hopefully, I have helped by sharing some light on the subject for those willing to continue the debate and to enlighten others. I will add, as I always say, "do what ever you feel is right and comfortable for you, as well as what ever work for you peacefully and successfully," as long as it does not hurt, harm or offend humankind. Know that there is no truth until you decide your own truth. However, before you make a definitive decision, always do your due diligent by thoroughly researching and investigating your subject matter of interest and only then are you able to refute or accept it. Then you are able to make a more informed decision that you feel comfortable with and ultimately able to live by. Remember and accept that we can never be separated from the presence, the power, the love and the goodness of the Almighty Divine Supreme Creator; except in your own thoughts. Once again, remember my standard phrase, "There is no truth until you decide your own truth."

EMPLOYMENT

Choosing the right career is one of the most critical decisions you will make during your life experience. It is said, "If you love your work, you will work for no pay." Choosing employment is an involved process that is based on a number of things such as, education, work-related values, personal skills, your personality, etc. There are times when a career development professional will use various tools to help you evaluate your interests, personality, skills and values; this is called a self-assessment. After the self-assessment, you will have a list of suitable careers you might want to select from. There are three basic common sense principles you should always follow for good decision-making:

1. Know yourself – this means you should know your strengths, values, personality and skills; this will help you make an intelligent choice that best fit you. Taking a career test will help to identify your personality types to determine your suitability; the careers that would be most promising to you and to learn detailed information about each one. This information can be invaluable for your professional growth, in that you learn more about yourself and identify your personal skills. In general, it will help you to understand yourself better, along with the aforementioned put forth in Chapter 1.

2. Know your options – It is essential to think of as many alternatives as you can and learn as much about each one. Making the right employment choice will help to optimize job satisfaction by conducting a critical analysis regarding likes and dislikes in advance before accepting a job.

3. Make a good decision – It is imperative to investigative and/or research the "company culture" in advance. This

investigation/research should include, but not be limited to just gathering information about the job description. It should include outlook for professional growth, salary, commission, etc. Then you are in the best position to make an intelligent decision based on your findings.

No one knows everything about choosing a professional career. However, many potential job seekers think they know the right way to go about choosing employment; but they frequently end up being dissatisfied. Here are ten myths about choosing a career:

- **Choosing a career is simple** – Actually, choosing a career is an involved process and you should give it the time it deserves. Career planning is a multi-step process that involves learning enough about yourself and the occupations that you are considering in order to make a well-informed decision.

- **A career counselor can tell me what occupation to choose** – A career counselor, or any other career development professional, cannot tell you what is best for you. He or she can provide you with guidance in choosing a career and can help facilitate your decision.

- **I cannot make a living from my hobby** – Says Who? When choosing a career, it makes perfect sense to choose one that is related to what you enjoy doing in your spare time. In addition people tend to become very skilled in their hobbies, even though most of the skill is gained informally. Once again, "If you love the work you are doing, you will do it without pay."

- **I should choose a career from a "Best Careers" list** – Every year, especially during milestone years, i.e. the beginning of a new decade, there are numerous articles and books that list what "the experts" predict will be "hot jobs." It cannot hurt to look at those lists to see if any of the careers on it appeal to you, but you should not use the list to dictate your choice. While the predictions are often based on valid data, sometimes things change. Most often what is hot this year will not be hot a few years from now. Also, you need to take into account your interest, values and skills when choosing a career. Just because the outlook for an occupation is good, it does not mean that occupation is right for you.

- **Making a lot of money will make me happy** – While salary is important, it is not the only factor you should look at when choosing a career. Countless surveys have shown that money does not necessarily lead to job satisfaction. For many people enjoying what they do at work is much more important. However, you should consider earnings, among other things, when evaluating an occupation.

- **Once I choose a career I will be stuck in it forever** – Not True. If you are unsatisfied in your career for any reason, you can always change it. You will be in good company, many people change careers several times over the course of their lifetimes.

- **If I change careers my skills will go to waste** – Your skills are yours to keep. You can take them from one job to another. You may not use them in the exact same way, but they should not go to waste (skills referred to here is different from "restraint of trade").

- **If my parents and/or siblings are good in a par-**

ticular field, I will be too – Everyone is different and what works for one-person want necessarily work for another, even if that other person is a family member with whom you have a lot in common. If a family member has a career that interest you, look into it, but be aware of the fact that it may not necessarily be a good fit for you.

- **All I have to do is choose an occupation...Things will fall into place after that** – Choosing a career is a great start, but there is a lot more to do after that. A Career Action Plan is a road map that takes you from choosing a career to becoming employed in that occupation to reaching your long-term career goals.

- **There is very little I can do to learn an occupation without actually working in it** – While first hand experience is great, there are other ways to explore an occupation. You can read about it either in print resources or online. You can also interview individuals working in that field.

Every employer looks forward in hiring top-notch employees for the betterment of their company; one's business acumen is essential. Therefore, an employer is looking to see what skills one may have when seeking employment. There are large numbers of unemployed people in our society today, including those who have been laid off from their previous work. Also, there are those who just graduated from college, so finding employees to work is not that difficult, the issue is finding the best one. It is no more than right for an employer to find an exemplary employee that will be an asset rather than a liability for the company. Most employers look for particular qualities in an employee such as:

1. **Talent and skill** – An applicant's educational background,

training and work experience are all major factors that an employer always considered. However, the decision is not solely based on the applicant's competency, school graduated from or the number of years previously worked. The employer is primary looking for someone who possesses the potential to be a great employee and help the company to grow.

2. **Productivity and Efficiency** – An employer is not only looking at the applicant's talent and/or skill; but that the applicant possesses the right kind of work ethic that would make him/her a productive and efficient employee. Further, the employer wants to know what the applicant's attitude and performance was like in previous employment and whether or not the applicant had the initiative to always give his/her best at all times.

3. **Honesty, Trustworthiness and Good Work Ethic** – An employer knows the most talented and skillful employee still would not make it as an employee of the year if he/she is not honest, trustworthy and does not have good work ethics. This is why from the start; most employers may want to know if the applicant has a criminal record. The employer wants to guard against hiring someone that could be involved in fraud, forgery, violence, sexual abuse or any other unscrupulous and malicious acts.

4. **Presentable Image** – As an employee, you represent the company so you must have a presentable image. It is not that the employer is expecting you to look like a model, but you are expected to be well groomed, properly dressed and have good manners.

5. **Emotionally Stable** – The employer does not expect his/her employee to burst into tears or explode into a hot vicious temper every time something negative is said about

his/her work. Sometimes an employer may want the applicant to take a psychological exam to determine their
emotional stability prior to hiring them.

6. **Dependability** – An employer wants to know that his/her
   employee will never let him/her down on completing an
   assigned task. The employer wants to expect the best results on time.

7. **Ability to Relate and Work Well with Others** – A company is generally composed of many employees, so it
   proper for an employer to choose an employee who will
   be able to work and relate well with others. The applicant
   needs to be someone who has a positive disposition about
   life and does not spend a lot of time gossiping or back-
   stabbing fellow coworkers.

8. **Professionalism** – An employer does not want an employee who will make up excuses for not doing a good
   job. The employer needs to be able to expect the employee will come to work even if he/she is feeling a little
   ill and will not bring home problems to work.

9. **Manageability** – An employee should never think he/she
   is better than his/her employer. An employer wants someone who can listen and follow instructions and not resort
   to doing the work their own way. The employer does not
   need someone who is difficult to train and manage.

10. **Passion for the Job** – A great employee should not work
    only for the paycheck, he/she should love the job and be
    concern about the affairs of the company.

Remember, when an employer is looking to hire an employee, it boils
down to whether the applicant has three main aspects: a great mind, a
passionate heart and a driven spirit.

On the other hand, employees have employment rights and
a reasonable expectation to work in a safe non-hostile environment.

An employer has the main responsibility to supply his/her employees with appropriate tools, equipment and technologies to do the job required. This will truly enable the employee who wants to do good work to succeed. As a convenience, an employer may offer an on-site cafeteria, ample parking and a fitness facility. Having these types of amenities will help morale, as well as produce a place where minds and spirits can grow and achieve. In addition, an employee expects the employer to promote a healthy work environment such as, having smoke-free areas throughout the work place and permits smoking only in designated areas. In this technological age, employees expect to have access to resources needed, proper workstation seating and computer usage to help maximize their comfort and productivity throughout their workday. It is reasonable for employees to expect to be provided resources, information and seminars on health and wellness topics, as well as the type of health benefits the employer will provide, if any. The topics may include information on parenting, Alzheimer's and adult care, financing a college education, healthy eating, nutrition counseling, etc. Also, the retirement plan should be explained to the employee in clear concise language, up to and including the employer's contributions to the plan.

An employee has the right to have proper communication when there is a change in his/her employment. Any kind of change in employment situation, whether in a personal setting, can create anxiety if not properly planned out, even though change is inevitable. An employee has the right to be given advance notice so he/she can make the necessary preparation for the change. Without proper notification, the employee can sometimes be left on-edge and create unhealthy stressful situation. This can also happen if the employee does not have sufficient time to adjust to the change with his/her family. However, changes in employee expectations do not need to create unhealthy stress, in fact change can actually be healthy. For example, provide the employee with resources in order to deal with the change, which can make the situation more manageable. These resources can include training, counseling support, sharing information and open communication. A common mistake made by the employer is not giving the employee a viable explanation for why the change is necessary. Sometimes the employer is hesitant in giving an explanation for the change because he/she thinks it will generate more questions then they want to answer; however avoidance only make the situation worse. Employers should anticipate and be willing to answer any questions raised by the employee. Planning for the change should include how to communicate the change to the employee, if the employer skips this step, the desired results may not be achieved. One important requirement of an employer is to have a well-written job description prepared for the employee. If the nature of the work changes, then a new job description should be developed and shared with the employee; this helps communicate what is expected of him/her. Ongoing communications are extremely important; employers should have regular schedule meetings with each employee so there is an avenue for the employer to share how they see the employee performance. Also, this venue will allow the employee to ask questions or make comments or suggestions concerning the work (the ultimate goal is to achieve a good job). An employee should receive a well thought out policies and procedure in writing via an Employee Handbook. This makes easier to communicate the company's policies because they are in text and can be cited for reference. Further, the Employee Handbook can tell the employees how they are expected to conduct themselves while they are working for the company. Also, it tells employees what they can expect from the company; providing this information keeps both employee and employer honest toward each other.

As previously stated, every employer has the utmost responsibility to provide a safe and secure work environment for his/her employee. No employee should be required to work in a hostile environment. A hostile work environment is primarily a legal term used to describe a workplace situation where an employee cannot reasonably perform his/her work, due to certain behaviors by management or co-workers that are deemed hostile. Hostility in this form is not only a boss being rude, yelling or annoying. It is very specific, especially in the setting when one is suing an employer for either wrongful termination or for creating an environment that causes severe stress to the employee. A hostile work environment is defined by any act of sexual harassment on the part of bosses or co-workers. Any acts or remarks that are overtly discriminatory regarding age, race, gender, sexual orientation or disability are also considered to create a hostile work environment. Also, a hostile work environment is when a boss or manager begins to engage in a manner designed to make you quit in retaliation for your actions. This could stem from an employee reporting safety violations; get injury at work; attempt to join an union; complain to upper level management about problems at work or act as a whistleblower. Overt hostility that threatens an employee physical well-being is also consider a hostile work environment. More over, as an employee you feel specifically threats or violent behavior level at you, this is not only hostile but also potentially criminal. When employees find themselves in a hostile work environment, they may not know how to act or what to do. Actions should be determined by the degree of hostility. Most companies have policies in place to deal with this type of behavior. However, when management fails to act appropriately, you can sue the company. Success in this type of lawsuit largely depends on not only how management failed to help but also how you acted. If you respond with hostility in a hostile work environment, chances are your lawsuit will be unsuccessful. Studies show that in court cases, the employee behavior is scrutinized as carefully as management's behavior. It is best, soon as possible, to make complaints about your manager to upper level management (to create a paper trial) or to contact government agencies that help employees with discrimination or poor treatment in the workplace. These agencies can vary from city to city and from state to state. A good place to start is the federal U.S. Department of Labor, which can direct you to these resources within your particular area. You may also consider working with attorneys that specialize in suing companies for these issues (be very selected in choosing an attorney). I suggest first check with free sources, since suing a company can be quite expensive, and should you lose, you may be responsible for lawyer's fees and court costs. Always do what you feel is right for you, after you have discussed the issue with a knowledgeable rational unemotional third party that have your best interest at heart.

There are generally no set rule for coworkers to date or not, however one must be aware of the pros and cons of employees dating. While dating a coworker might seem like a wild, adventurous thrill ride that could make an otherwise drab workweek much more exciting; however there are a few key factors to take in consideration before taking the plunge into an office romance.

- **Office size** – A small to medium size office can be a potentially disastrous place to find oneself attached to a coworker. While falling for a coworker is not necessarily advisable in any office environment, this is even more so true in a small workplace where everyone is into everyone else's business (both personal and work-related). Conversely, it is only natural to find yourself attracted to someone you work with closely day in and day out. While larger offices are generally more impersonal, smaller offices tend to create the type of closeness that can lead to the development of a romantic relationship.

- **The work place can create right conditions** – When getting involved with a coworker, chances are that you can bypass all the intricate steps that are generally required during the courtship, in terms of attracting and impressing the person in the beginning. You are already in direct contact with him or her on a daily basis, you are able to talk about life and work, and perhaps you have lunch and coffee breaks together. This almost as if all the early stages of the courting/dating game have been completed.

- **To chance or not to chance** – Ask yourself, "at what point do I decide if it is worth my while?" Well, before you make any drastic decisions, you should weigh all the potential benefits and disasters that could be associated with your decision. After which, you can make the decision unemotionally to determine if it outweighs the price you may have to pay.

- **The benefits** – With any new relationship, the real excitement comes in the early stages such as: flirting, the secret e-mails, the smiles, sexual glances, the playful jokes, letters and cards. These are all bonuses that will most definitely bring joy to your long hard working day at the office. Other benefits, you may feel vitalized when you wake up in the morning, you cannot wait to see him or her in their office attire with a sexy smile when you walk in the office. Perhaps there might even be a little good morning peck on the cheek or even the mouth. If she is the office babe or he is the office hunk, chances are you will feel and act like the office queen or stud with this new boost of excitement in your life experience.

- **The downsides** – As with everything in life, along with the good comes the bad. The only difference in this case is that when it is bad, it can be horrible.

When things are not going well at work, whether it is a personal issue or a work-related incident, the last thing you need is added pressure stemming from tension between you and your office flame. That cold, hard stare he or she can give you will really burn a hole right through the back of your brain when tension arises. Even worse is when others around the office have to witness this chaos, it is not pleasant in the least, nor is it good for your image in the office. Furthermore, the more private time you spend with your office flame during office hours, the more and more you will begin to alienate yourself from your other coworkers. The worst thing you can do is distance yourself from your immediate associates, especially those you have developed personal working relationships with. As soon as trouble in corporate paradise rears its ugly head and you find yourself as the office outsider, you will have to work overtime to regain their trust and friendship once again. When the going gets tough, it is difficult to avoid one another in a small office. Chances are your office space or workstation is just around the corner from his or hers, so attempting to ignore him or her all week is virtually impossible. If he or she is having a bad day, guess who will be first in line to hear about it all day at work, then some more during your private time. If he or she has mood swings, you are enemy number one. However, in a larger office, you may be able to pull it off.

- **The breakup** – As with many relationships, you may find that this one is not simply working. Should you decide that it is time to break it off, those 40 work hours per week might feel like an eternity in the early stages of the breakup. The beauty of breaking off a relationship with someone not your coworker is that you no longer have to see him or her afterward. Obviously, the same rules do not apply when it comes to an office fling. Further, if you are responsible for ending it, he or she might seek revenge and try to make your life miserable at work. Do not let it be your boss, he or she might just get you fired. At worse, jealousy might take its toll when you witness him or her flirting with other coworkers, going out on lunch dates and ultimately moving on with their life without you. Such distractions can seriously harm your work performance. And last but not least, if you gossiped about other coworkers with him or her by bad-mouthed anyone during your good times together, there is a chance that those comments will come back to haunt you.

I tried to outline some of the pros and cons of dating a co-worker by arming you with some information to help you make a wise professional decision. If you find yourself in this type of predicament, do what you feel is right for you, but first take your emotions out of it and let your brain rationally weigh the pros and cons and then make the decision. A word of warning to the wise, unless you honestly believe that you can juggle your career and a relationship with your coworker, you might want to do yourself a favor and keep your business and personal life separate.

RETIREMENT

Retirement is a reward for having worked for a required number of years, which is a major goal most people seek to achieve in their life experience. It is generally a long exciting time coming that is why it is important to prepare and seek advice before retiring. Retirement is a big decision, a lot people do not take into consideration when and where they should retire. They have worked hard for many years, waiting for the day or the year that they are able to retire and live the easy life. In your eagerness, you must take the time and make your retirement as easy and as stress-free as possible. Once you retire choosing the right city is a big step too, it is probably not a very good idea to move to a city you do not know anything about and have never visited. There are some states that do not require retirees to file state income taxes, which could be a saving to you. Knowing when to retire is a very difficult decision, lots of factors come into play, which does not just effect the person retiring. Something this important affects the retiree's family, as well. The following are some things to consider for retirement:

1. Seek good advice and conduct your own research to find out when retiring is for you. A retirement calculator can help you run scenarios. You can run a few different time scenarios to get a prognosis of when will be the best time for you to retire.

2. Keep your theories traditional, do not postulate that stocks will sky rocket and you can get some big cash out. This will help leave room for error, so you will not be disappointed when investments do not give you as high of return as you would like.

3. Know if you are entitled to receive social security or not. If you are eligible to receive social security, know when the best time to opt for it. Generally, you are eligible at age 62, providing you have the required number of credits; however at age 65 your social security benefits are greater. If you are under 55 years of age, assume that you will not be getting as much as retired people get today. The social security program is facing some financial issues right now,

so run your retirement scenarios accounting for a 25-percent to 75-percent cut in social security and see where you are.

4. Handle your expenses by eliminating or reducing debt, try to become debt free as you can. Have aspirations to pay off your credit in full each month.

5. Obtain a surplus, which means that your expenses are less than your income. Once you have gained a surplus, put it into a saving or a 401K plan through your employer.

6. Invest in things like stocks and mutual funds wisely. Do not use investment services that require commissions and large fees in order to invest. Put money into investments yourself and make decisions on your own to avoid fees. This will add two percent to your investments and help you to retire earlier.

The above plan of action can serve as a great road map to guide you toward a successful retirement. You do not want to retire from one job only to have to find work elsewhere in order to make ends meet. I personally recommend starting your retirement planning five to seven years prior to actually retiring, if not much sooner. Here are some additional things you should know before you retire:

- **Leave your work behind the right way** – Individual wanting to retire usually do not walk into work one day and decide their retirement will start tomorrow. As previously stated, retiring from work may require careful planning and preparation. You may have to work closely with someone to train them on your duties. If you own your own business, slowly phase out your current clients and stop taking new clients. Ending things the right way at work will help pave your way to a relaxing retirement.

- **Think about lifestyle changes** – When you retire

you must make adjustments to your lifestyle. A retiree should analyze monthly expenses to determine that your monthly budget covers everything. As a retiree you may no longer be able to afford the same lifestyle, you may have to decide what things to give up or how to find the extra income to afford everything.

• **Determine the source of your income** – Some retirees have been saving for years for their retirement. You may have a 401K or pension plan that will provide you all the money you need for a long retirement. Some retirees are able to live off their social security; others sell their home or other properties and move to a less expensive location. It is important to start planning as soon as possible by seeking the guidance from a financial advisor or someone you trust who can help you better understand your finances during retirement.

• **Fill your days with things you enjoy** – Many retirees look forward to doing one thing and only one thing when they retire, absolutely nothing. After years of working hard, you can understand why. However, once retirement begins, a retiree may soon realize he/she needs something to help pass the time. They may find new hobbies or interests: like golf, exercise classes, cooking, etc. Some retirees enjoy having the time to spend with friends, family members and/or grandchildren. Retirees who do not have any thing to do may become bored and/or depressed. Planning activities during retirement can help to make the most of their retirement years.

• **Plan for health care cost** – The rising cost of health

care is an issue for many retirees. No one can predict the type of health care they will need in the future. Some companies offer retirees excellent health care benefits. Others rely on Medicare or supplemental health insurance that they pay extra for every month. These costs should be included in monthly expenses when planning for retirement. Also, there are certain things like long-term care that are not covered by insurance. Retirees will have to think about how they will pay for long-term care or other unforeseen health care costs.

These are just a few retirement things you should know. In addition, I suggest that you have several conversations with several different retirees and seek their words of wisdom on this all-important subject. If you plan your retirement right, it can and will be the most exciting and enjoyable time in your golden years.

The following are my *Wardisms* on the subject of "LIFE:"

Your life experience should be comparable
to having played in the super bowl of life
and won MVP (most valuable player).

Always augment your options, then you
will not have to look back and wonder why.

Do not define yourself by your confinement;
life has to much for you to fine and refine.

Do not define yourself by your confinement;

You are admired and known by your good
deeds, not by your religious needs or creeds.

Do not restrain, contain or detain yourself
from receiving your good in life, always
sustain and maintain so you can obtain.

Being free is your birthright, it cost no fee
so let everyone be the way they choose to see.

When you steal your way through life, you
have no zeal nor can you seal a real deal.

To positively orchestrate your life experience,
you must take a stand with a well thought out
plan, marinated in meditation and prayer.

Allow your negative past to pass from you
fast, then you can live a happy life at last.

Never refrain to train yourself; work hard you
will gain your fame and your life experience
will not be in vain and you want be shamed.

Do not lock me in a box; I have many skills,
I am sharp-witted like a fox.

Be bold and put your soul in accomplishing
your life goals, so you may forever hold.

To stand up, you do not need a rope, definitely
not dope, just a little hope will keep you from
sliding down life's slippery slope.

When you firmly set your sights on your life
plight, your zeal will not let you loss the deal.

W

Keep your own pace while running life race,
ultimately you will find your place.

W

Your plan must have a purpose for you to
get a chance to take your stance.

W

Be patience, slow down and be at peace with
yourself, as well as your Creator. Also relax,
be gentle and respectful to yourself. Just
be happy and kind, because after all it is not
really that serious leave the mess behind.

W

Stop jiving, stay alive, look alive, then you
will not have to take a dive.

W

Division without vision has no provision.

W

Protection does not need correction when you
are headed in the right direction.

W

Peal off your phony seal, be real and allow your
body, mind and spirit to truly heal.

W

Have the guts to leave your hut and get off your butt
to get out of your lazy rut.

W

I have come of age as a seasoned person with a definite purpose and reason for this season.

W

When you are right hold up your bright light, be firm
in your stance, then you will always win out over
might without a struggle or fight.

Be the master of your craft like a sailor of his raft,
then you will not have to gain by graft.

You should always do good in your neighbor-
hood focusing on the less fortune if you would.

In life, your ace is to always have a plan in
place, then there is no problems you cannot face or
be out in space.

Live your life at a steady comfortable pace by always maintaining your space, when you get to your
place, you will surely know you have won the race.

I am free of all my outstanding debts, having lost
very few bets and never got caught up in life's mess.

When you sow good seeds and do good deeds,
the universe will meet your needs.

Stay in good health so you can work and
enjoy your wealth.

Do not jive around on your nine to five.

By playing at work, might keep you from
receiving your full day's pay.

When you get tired at work still give your
best, stay wired and you will not get fired.

Always be the best employee on your job and
you will not have to worry about the rest.

When you are in the work place, always
respect your co-workers' working space.

When you carve out your niche in life, you have
eased your strife.

Do not haze and faze others, be willing to lend support to your sisters and brothers.

By omitting
you end up committing
because you did not admit.

Do not fret, I have no regrets about how I
lived my life experience.

Do not hate your fate, participate and make
it great for your sake.

Why be in doubt, move forward and figure
it out, so you can jump and shout.

Do not move slow,
you will lose your flow
and end up with no place to go.

Nothing in life remains the same, so you must
change and not blame and/ or complain.

W

Stay engaged and conquer life maze.

W

In your life experience, you must recognize
when the bottom line is the bottom line.

W.

To run life's race successfully, you must
put your own plan of action in place,
then you have dealt your winning ace.

W

Seriousness means you must truly live
your life experiences unadulterated
seriously.

W

When things in your life get hazy just
maintain your sanity and do not get lazy
and start acting crazy.

W

Do not always tell silly jokes be serious
and give people hope with positive strokes.

W

Girls and boys never ever let anyone take
your joy and play with it like a toy.

W

You are now being told that it gets old
chasing a pot of gold to the end of a
rainbow, which is not there to behold.

In closing, this chapter on "Life," can serve as a life-message for each of us to govern ourselves and live out our life experiences. However, it is of extreme importance that we must learn to treat all humankind, as we would like to be treated and to live our lives by the laws of the universe and the fruits of the Spirit. Then we will develop, build and create a more humane civilized peaceful world for all of us to live our life experiences and for generations to come. The fruits of the Spirit are: love, joy, peace, patience, kindness, goodness, faithfulness, gentleness and self-control:

- *LOVE* is that magnetic, attractive force that binds together the whole human family. It has been called the "great healer."

- *JOY* has been referred to as the happiness of the Almighty Divine Supreme Creator expressed through the perfect idea; humanity. Joy is strength giving and a healing power.

- *PEACE* is a positive assurance that only the good is true. When we have peace within, external events rarely disturb that "calm peacefulness of the soul."

- *PATIENCE* is that powerful attitude of mind that is often characterized by poise, serenity, inner calmness and quiet endurance.

- *KINDNESS* is one of the gentle expressions of love that may be shared with all of creation. There may be room for expansion of both giving and receiving greater loving kindness, which could make a tremendous difference in the quality of our lives

- *GOODNESS* is more then simply refraining from doing harm. It is a definite positive awareness of the Almighty Divine Supreme Creator's unfailing perfection, which allows problems to disappear as darkness before light.

- *FAITHFULNESS* is living life anchored in the invisible, the real and the truth. Faithfulness includes unfailing assurance, confidence and strength through which we overcome the circumstances of the world.
- *GENTLENESS* is a tremendous aid to growing in wisdom, compassion and having inner, as well as outer vision. It is undisturbed by the clamor, noise and confusion that may reign around us. Rather it brings calmness, quietness and humility in our life experiences.
- *SELF-CONTROL* is truly the starting point of all control in our life experiences. Through prayer and quiet reflection (meditation) life begins to take on deeper meaning and then we know we have the ability to take charge of our own personal life experiences.

Remember to be in control without any power is like a bird's feather trying to find stability in a windstorm. We must continue to cultivate these fruits of Spirit into our life experiences in order to bring them into abundant harvest. Then our life experiences will be blessed with equal measure filled with life's treasures. We must always give in order to receive our life blessing. Therefore, it is best to always make good-large deposits in life's bank; because we cannot make good withdrawals if we have not made good deposits therein.

LIFE IS A GREAT AWESOMELY BEAUTIFUL GIFT TO BE-
HOLD!
TO THYSELF BE TRUE

3
RELATIONSHIP

It is important to develop and have a quality relationship with another in order to live a productive, happy and peaceful life. Our relationships are only as healthy as we are mentally, physically, emotionally and spiritually. It would be very hard to have a meaningful relationship with another if he/she has not clearly matured mentally, physically, emotionally and spiritually. Who needs "child's play" or what others may call "puppy love." There are no clearly defined ways to develop a quality relationship, however it would be helpful in using the right words or giving the right gift or even using the right perfume to make it happen. Relationships are an intrigue part of our daily living and life progression. A loving relationship must be predicated upon togetherness, connectedness, inseparability and interdependence. It must have love and respect as its motivating factor and not selfness and unhappiness. He/she must recognize the good qualities his/her mate possesses and not look for or focus on their negativity. [Throughout this chapter, I will use the words: *mate, partner and significant other,* interchangeable]. Remember the relationship becomes what you want it to become, good or bad. First, to truly love someone else, you must lose your ego. This is absolutely essential in having a meaningful relationship. Also, it is equally critical in maintaining and continually improving your relationship once you are already in it. Nothing will kill a relationship, even the best of relationships, more quickly than when one's ego getting in the way. The following are five ways your ego can ruin your relationship and how to avoid letting it happen:

1. When our ego is on guard, we must resist the temptation to defend ourselves. Think about the number of times you have fought with your mate and when things get a little heated and you start to defend yourself. All you hear is yourself being attacked and you immediately go into a "defensive mode." Do you know when you defend yourself in a fight, what is really happening is that you are defending your ego. Also, it means you have stopped listening to your mate. When your mate tells you that they do not like the way you have been acting lately, you should hear them out instead of defending yourself. Invariably, it will almost always create a much better outcome.

2. To truly love your mate, you must separate your ego from yourself. This is also true if you want to be able to totally love yourself. Even though we are all ego-driven to some extent or another; so let us acknowledge it and embrace the fact that we need to detach our egos. This will help to cultivate and maintain a truly amazing relationship with our mates.

3. Our egos hate feedback no matter how much we prepare, plan and hope for a good conversation with our significant other. Our egos are the one thing that will consistently ruin any conversation we are about to have, if we let it. There are times when your mate might have some things to say to you that you would rather not hear. But in order to maintain a healthy relationship, do not allow your ego to get in the way from hearing your mate out.

4. Our egos are always active, so we must be willing to get rid of our egos and have a healthy relationship. If you want to have a meaningful relationship with your partner and go to the next level, you must take your ego out of the equation. By getting rid of your ego does not change who you are, it just helps you to be a better listener without being defensive.

5. Your ego will cause you to hurl hurtful comments at your significant other. So the next time you see your ego getting involved in your relationship, get rid of it. Also, if you find yourself defending your position or not allowing yourself to really listen, then you need to take a step back and listen carefully to what is really being said. This can create a healthy and a most meaningful relationship.

It is best for both partners to leave their egos outside their home before entering, so it will not become a weapon used to destroy their relationship. It is important that we learn how to suppress our individual egos and better yet replace them with the universal ego (being together as one). A relationship that lives on love and respect has longevity because love and hate cannot coexist in the same place. In our relationships love has no other desire than to fulfill its destiny of love, so leave out the ego, it serves no honorable purpose.

Our supreme desire is to love and be loved, it is extremely important to our growth and survival. Love is essential in our relationship, to give love to another is to give them power to conquer their need to live and to be apart of worldly activities. We all desire peace, love, romance and beauty in our lives, as well as joy in our hearts and in our homes. The Almighty Divine Supreme Creator made man and woman equal pairs in order for them to unite and procreate. It was intended that men would have aggressive and progressive qualities to construct the world and their homes; but to be balanced by women qualities that gives cohesiveness of love to the world and their homes. Clearly, the world-families-homes can only endure by balancing the male-female qualities. A happy peaceful, loving home is one where the husband, wife and children will think of each other first before him or herself. Also, they will unequivocally give freely without motive or self-gain. Furthermore, in a loving peaceful happy family each family member will go out of his or her way to serve the other in order to make sure they are happy and conversely will refrain from doing anything to make a family member unhappy. This should be the norm, not just a concept. It is extremely important to always see the problems, issues, disagreements and/or misunderstanding you have with your mate by viewing them from the eyes of your mate. In other words put yourself in your mate's place then you are better able to understand what your mate is thinking and/or feeling.

The word relationship takes on many meanings in our life experiences, such as with a spouse, a significant other, a friend, a family member and others. The dictionary defines relationship as:

1. The condition or fact of being related; connection or association.
2. Connection by blood or marriage; kinship.
3. A particular type of connection existing between people related to or having dealings with each other; a close relationship with siblings.
4. A romantic or sexual involvement.

In addition to the above dictionary definition of relationship, I believe every time we connect with another person we establish a relationship. I emphasize the word, connect, because a relationship can be established or at least initiated by a look, a touch, a verbal communication, etc. Initiating or establishing a relationship does not make for a complete relationship. A relationship is like an electrical wire or a two-way road. I liken it to a double pipeline with one pipe belonging to each participant in the relationship. Through each of these pipes emits either a positive or negative flow at any given time. A positive flow represents giving, outgoing, unselfishness, service and/or love. A negative flow represents taking, selfishness, abuse and/or hate. Like electrical flow in a wire or traffic flow on a road that flow can fluctuate in speed, strength and intensity. This means one part of the relationship can range widely within either a positive direction or the negative direction. This could be from a kind word to a deep abiding love and admiration, or from careless hurtfulness to a deadly hatred. It could run the full gamut of positive to negative. A good relationship is where both partners are flowing in a positive direction. On the other hand, a bad relationship is where both partners are flowing in a negative direction. A dysfunctional relationship is when one partner is flowing in a positive direction and the other partner is flowing in a negative direction. We can agree that the word relationship means the joining together of spouses and significant others by marriage or otherwise.

My wife, Gwendolyn "Gwen" Pothier Ward coined the word, "WELATIONSHIP." **(This word is licensed under the Creative Com- mons, the license allows for redistribution, commercial and non-commercial, as long as it is passed along unchanged and in whole, with credit to Gwen).** My lovely wife, Gwen coined the word to replace or to be used in conjunction with the word relationship. She states, "If spouses and significant others would see their relationship as a welationship, it could change their thinking and the way they receive and share love with each other." Gwen adds, "that words have a significant impact on our minds, in that we receive messages subliminally on a subconscious level." Subliminal is defined, when a message is received below the threshold of consciousness without the person being fully aware of the change, stimuli, image, etc. Gwen and I clearly believe that words create thoughts and thoughts create actions and actions create changes. The word, "we" indicates togetherness and connectedness. When you are together in love with your spouse or significant other, it can unquestionably be called welationship. The prefix, "re" denotes: return, redo, repeat, replace, repair, etc.; so subliminally by using the word, relationship we might think it is permissible to keep returning, repeating replacing, repairing, etc. from one relationship to another. So just maybe, if we were to substitute the word welationship for the word relationship, it might subliminally readjust and change our thought process regarding the way we interact with our spouses and significant others. By thinking we are in a welationship, as oppose to relationship, it might keep us together, connected and reduce the divorce rate, which is hovering around 50 percent.

Several people marry more than once, which we might think that we are terrible at figuring out how to have a long-term lovely marriage. A typical marital pattern starts with one or both persons falling head-over-heels for each other, with all its heat-thumping, starry-eyed craziness subsequently proclaiming being in love. However, it takes only a little while before the fog dissipates and the real object of desire comes into focus. In some cases, the truth does not set in until after the marriage. After the marriage, all the hidden idiosyncrasies, bad habits, snoring, etc. are noticed. Then one morning you wake up with the person sleeping next to you wearing your wedding ring. It has been said that more energy, time, effort and money go into preparing for the wedding rather than planning for a meaningful happy marriage, as well as working toward making it last. Someone was said hilariously, that once the bride and groom eat some of the wedding cake, they lose their libido. Before a couple pursues marriage, they should establish how important their relationship [welationship] is to them. They should ask themselves is it just for a moment or is it something we want to see blossom into a long-term meaningful relationship [welationship] and ultimately marriage. Knowing and fully understanding a meaningful relationship [welationship] takes much work. They should agree to and incorporate the following steps to work toward having a meaningful committed relationship [welationship]:

- Having a open mind to change your opinions
- Willing to give of yourself and others
- Identifying the need to adapt
- Complimenting each other
- Being willing to accept the little things that do not matter. For instance, leaving the toilet seat up after using the rest room or eating out instead of cooking dinner.
- Spending quality time together (couple that plays together, stays together)
- Supporting each other (being each others cheerleader)
- Coming to a mutual agreement with each other when there is no right or wrong answer and knowing when to just let it go (compromising)
- Flirting with each other (not only at home even in the public)
- Treating each other with respect (being gentle and kind toward each other)
- Respecting each other's space (distance makes the heart grow fonder)
- Remember your manners such as: please, thank you, you are welcome, etc.
- Variety is the spice of life (try it you might like something different)
- Known that two heads are better than one
- Laughing together is good medicine
- When the going gets tough, the tough gets going (do not give up)

All relationships [welationships] are not the same. What works for one couple may not work for the other; but consistent and the above proven techniques are the keys to having a good relationship [welationship]. However, some people embark upon a relationship with the intent of only fulfilling their personal needs and/or desires. Once their needs and/or desires are satisfied they sever the relationship. This is usually done because it was not grounded in being a welationship (togetherness; connectedness). The following story exemplifies this kind of relationship:

> A young lady hated herself because she was blind.
> She hated everyone but her loving boyfriend. He was always there for her to protect and console her. One day she told her boyfriend, "If I were not blind and could see the world I would be very happy and I would marry you." Sometime later, a pair of eyes was donated to her. When the bandages were removed, she was able to see everything, as well as her ever present boyfriend. He asked her, "Now that you can see the world are you happy and will you marry me?" The young lady looked at her boyfriend and saw that he was blind. The sight of his closed eyelids shocked her. She had not expected that. The thought of looking at his blindness for the rest of her life led her to refuse to marry him. Her boyfriend was emotionally hurt, he left in tears. Days later he sent her an e-mail saying, "Take good care of your eyes, my dear, for before they were yours, they were mine.

This is how relationships are when they are not founded upon a welationship; often they change their positions. Some mates forget what life was like before, as well as who was always by their side in the most painful situations. Remember life is a beautiful gift filled with love and having a committed relationship/welationship with your mate. You and your mate can share a meaningful welationship (togetherness; connectedness) by being mindful of the following:

- Before you speak an unkind word to your mate, think of someone who cannot speak.

- Before you complain about your mate's cooking, think of someone who has nothing to eat.
- Before you complain about your spouse, think of someone who is crying out for a *WELATIONSHIP*.
- Before you complain about your children, think of someone who desires children but are barren.
- Before you argue about a dirty house with your spouse, think of those who are homeless.
- Before you complain to your spouse about your job, think of the number of unemployed people.
- When you think of depressing thoughts, just put a smile on your face, give your mate a big hug and say, "I love you and glad we have a *WELATION-SHIP*."

In a study published in the July 2009 Journal, *Psychological Science,* Northwestern University, by psychologist Daniel Molden, her research looked at the possible differences between the way dating and married couples see each other. The research consists of 92 dating couples and 77 married couples to complete questionnaire about satisfaction with their relationship. The questionnaires revealed, not surprising, that marriage changes things. The research showed that everyone married or dating thinks the best partner is the one who acts as a cheering section and brings out his or her best. But that type of relationship only translates into a truly happy marriage when the partner seems to accept a real commitment and helps in the day-to-day obligations as a couple. The surprise was the switch from the focus on the "me" to a focus on the "we." For example, going from the first blush of love to picking up someone else's underwear off the floor (lack of welationship). What really stands out in the research is the idea that satisfaction within any relationship [welationship] is based on perception rather than actual fact and therein lies the rub of not only love, but also of living with someone on intimate terms. Molden's study focuses on the person's "perception" of the other person, not the reality of the situation. If we perceive our partner to be supportive of our goals, we are happy. If we perceive a spouse as committed to the family, we are even happier. Although, the researcher points to the change in the focus of perception from self to the couple as an indicator of a good or bad marriage. However the real problem for love is the very fact of projecting everything on another person, no matter the focus. We seem to think we are very good at knowing one another, but the truth is our personal agendas get in the way of really knowing our mates. As self-interested, self-absorbed creatures, our own thoughts, feelings, needs and goal come first at the expense of not considering the thoughts, feelings, needs, and goals of our partner's. I frequently say if we were to see our welationship form the eyes of our partner's, we will not become disillusion by our own illusion. Happy marriages are when both partners respect each other in a loving sweet-natured way, even when things are not so great. We know that happiness is a state of mind, however when we work toward having a welationship (togetherness; connectedness), it becomes our reality. Then our reality becomes a blissful welationship that can and will withstand any marital storm.

MARRIAGE

We know that the concept of marriage has not always been the way it is traditionally viewed today. The Romans had a very interested view toward marriage – *"matrimonia debent esse libera,"* translated to mean, marriages ought to be free. This meant that either spouse could opt out of the marriage if things were not working out for them. However, Victorian England had a vastly different view, in that people got married and stayed together for better or for worse. The society frowned on divorce and divorced people were likely to find themselves as social pariahs. Presently, both the aforementioned view exists in our society. With globalization being what it is today, the so called "backward" countries are catching up with the so called "progressive" countries, because women have access to higher education and higher salaries are much less willing to comply with traditional roles and expectations. No divorcee enjoys the agony that it induces; conversely, no one wants to bear the pain of being in an uncomfortable corrosive marriage. In such case, splitting up is preferable than staying together for the children seek or to keep up social appearances. However, it is predicated on the kind of relationship you have with your spouse. Be mindful that some relationships, providing if they were established as a welationship, are worth working at; conversely, some are not. The lists below are some frequently cited reasons why marriages end in divorce courts:

- Lack of commitment to the marriage
- Lack of communication between spouses
- Infidelity
- Abandonment
- Alcohol Addiction
- Substance Abuse
- Physical Abuse
- Sexual Abuse
- Emotional Abuse
- Inability to manage or resolve conflict
- Personal differences or irreconcilable differences
- Differences in personal and career goals
- Financial problems
- Different expectations about household tasks
- Different expectations about having or rearing children
- Interference from parents or in-laws
- Lack of maturity
- Intellectual incompatibility
- Sexual incompatibility

- Insistence of sticking to traditional roles and not allowing room for personal growth
- Falling out of love
- Religious conversion or religious beliefs
- Cultural and lifestyle differences
- Inability to deal with each other's petty idiosyncrasies
- Mental instability or Mental illness
- Criminal behavior and incarceration for crime

When we look at the research done on the causes of divorce, the following results were reported:

1. Lack of communication is one of the leading causes of divorce. A marriage is on the rocks when the lines of communication fail. You cannot have an effective relationship if neither one of you does not want to discuss your feelings regarding the problem(s). When you do not discuss openly your personal or mutual problem(s) with your mate resentment will simmer with you expecting your spouse to guess what the problem is about, in most instances to no avail. Remember no one is a mind reader, not even your spouse. Communication is a two-way process.

2. Divorces often happen because people rarely discuss their expectations in detail prior to marriage and are less willing to work on their marriages afterwards. Also they would like to have quick solutions rather than actual resolving problem. People have gotten divorced for trivial reasons like snoring, arguing about leaving the toilet set up and the other partner wanted it left down, leaving dishes in the sink, toilet tissue not placed in the holder the way one partner wanted, etc., etc., etc.

3. People who come from divorced homes are more likely to get divorced than people who come from happily

married households. Divorce does not seem to be a big deal to those individuals who watched their parents go through one before.

4. People who get married between the ages of 23-27 are more likely to stay together than people who get married in their teens.

5. People who cohabit before marriage have higher rates of divorce than people who do not cohabit before marriage.

6. In many cases, few of the problems that cause divorce existed in the couple's relationship long before they even get married. The problems were either not acknowledged or were ignored in the fond hope that marriage might offer a miraculous panacea; well guess what, generally it does not. No one can make you feel better about yourself and you cannot change and save anyone. Know that you cannot change another person mind, ways and/or their actions; you can only change or rearrange your thoughts about the person and/or their action.

Until couples realize that it simply takes two wholes to make a lovable harmonious marriage and not two halves, they will continue to experience the above and contribute to the high divorce rate.

I would be extremely remiss if I did not offer some tips for saving your marriage and how to make it more lovable and harmonious. First, it is of paramount importance to know that marriage is not a game to be played. Once you wear the wedding ring, you must commit yourself to your partner whole heartily. Also, you must be ready to take all chances with that chosen person. Here are some tips to help save your marriage and to help you stay true to the wedding vows you made in front of the altar or wherever, as well as keep you out of divorce court:

1. *Acceptance* – It is always a wise move to learn and ac-

cept that it is a reality that problems will exist in the marriage and with your partner. Both partners should be realistic and honest enough to identify and accept the differences in the relationship [welationship] that may exist. The problems should be discuss openly, kindly and honestly so you can accept them and be ready to face the consequences together that may lie ahead.

2. *Talk, Talk, Talk* – Talking always helps in the relationship [welationship] it is paramount for married couples. Do not ever be afraid to talk your problems out. Talking will help both partners to understand the problem(s), thereby making it easy to compromise and to decide what to change and what should remain the same. If you sense that something is not right with your partner or the marriage, then make your partner aware of it and do not leave each in the dark. Also, it is good to air out things especially those that you would want known in the relationship [welationship], this will keep your partner from guessing. Your partner must be able to express his or her ideas, judgments and emotions. Talking helps both partners to know and understand each other's points of view. Try it; you have nothing to lose and every thing to gain.

3. *Renew Your Love For Each Other* – When you are married, it does not necessarily mean that you should stop dating each other. You should remain as respectful, sweet and loving when you are married like it was in your boy/girlfriend phase. When you renew your love for each other you do the kind of things you enjoyed doing prior to getting married. Some of those things can be going out on a date, watching a move together, go on a weekend vacation or for a month, shut out from the

world and just let your partner be the center of your attention. This will make your partner feel special. Also, surprise him or her with flowers, a gift, a card, etc., etc., etc. Then your partner will become the pleasure to your eyes and the treasure to you heart.

4. *Be Persistent* – I know dealing with marital problems can be uncomfortable and very stressful, but marriage is not promised to be a bed of roses. There are many obstacle married couples may face but as things get worse, do not easily give up. Be persistent and be optimistic with your relationship [welationship]. Always think the problem(s) can be solved and make a strong effort to do so. Do not just give up that easily, if one attempt of solving it fails, then try another one. Keep others out of your welationship.

5. *Seek The Right Advice* – Be cautious and not seek advice from someone who does not have your best interest at heart. Beware of seeking advice from family members they might favor one partner over the other. Their advice might be questionable at best. If you think the two of you cannot solve your conflict(s) alone, always seek good advice. I recommend seeking out an unattached third party who has nothing to gain or loss from either partner. However, my strongest preference is to seek out a profession marital counselor that both partners mutually agree to be counseled by.

6. *Keep Your Promise* – Whenever you say something to your spouse, you have to keep it and stand up for it. Do not be shaken by petty arguments, as these are just small tests in your married life. You have to show your partner you are capable of keeping your word. Then you will not lose the trust from your spouse easily. Trust is

a key element in your relationship [welationship], once you lose it; it is very hard to gain it back.

7. *Do Not Be Judgmental* – Being judgmental, jealous or having a nasty attitude can blind you from really respecting the true essence of your partner. When you are jealous of your partner, you will develop perverse feelings that can lead to false judgments. You should avoid being a jealous husband or a jealous wife, you must trust your partner and never judge him or her without a factual cause. If you cannot help from feeling jealous, then discuss why you are feeling jealous with your partner. Do not reach your own conclusion about the situation, until after you have had an honest discussion with your partner. Tell your partner that you are feeling jealous and then your partner can assure you that there is nothing to be worried about. Never create your own impressions out of your own instincts. When you learn to trust your partner, you will never feel jealous no matter what. Trust will give you peace of mind.

8. *Keep your marital finances current* – Establishing a budget is of paramount importance to the stability of the marriage. A budget can help to keep the bills current accumulated by both partners. Financial problems can lead to many other problems and concerns in a marriage if not handle appropriately.

9. *Keep the sexual light on* – Having sex with your partner was designed to produce pure, righteous, clean, holy and rich blessings. It is made to be the loving bond to preserve your marriage in love. Use it as an energizing magnet to draw you closer together with increasing love to heal over those little irritations in life. Always be giving, never selfish, in sex.

If married couples follow these tips, they should see a great improvement in their marriage. In addition, be mindful of the study by researchers, Dr. Rebecca Kippen and Professor Bruce Chapman from the Australian National University entitled, *What's Love Got To Do With It*. They identify what it takes to keep a couple together and they concluded it takes a lot more than just being in love. The study tracked nearly 2,500 couples, married or living together, from 2001 to 2007 to identify factors associated with those who remained together compared with those divorced or separated. The study found that a husband who is nine years older than his wife is twice as likely to get divorced, as do husbands who get married before they turn 25. Also, the study showed that children influence the longevity of a marriage or relationship. Further it showed that one-fifth of couples who have children before marriage; either from a previous relationship or in the same relationship separated; compared to just nine percent of couples without children born before marriage. In the study, it reveals that women who want children much more than their partners are also more likely to get a divorce. The study added, that a couple's parents relationship play an important factor in their own relationship. It shows that 16 percent of men and women whose parents separated or divorced experienced marital separation themselves, compared to 10 percent for those whose parents did not separate. Not surprisingly, the study showed, money also plays a role. It concluded that 16 percent of respondents who indicated they were poor or where the husband, not the wife, was unemployed had separated; compared with only nine percent of couples with healthy finances. Smokers are also a likely factor why a relationship ends in failure. Factors that were found to not significantly affect separation risk included the number and the age of children born to a married couple, as well as the wife's employment status and the number of years the couple had been employed. However, the true essence of any marriage (couple with the above) is to always treat your spouse the way you would like to be treated, as well as to see things from their perspective. Then your marriage will have a much greater chance for success. Always be the voice of reasoning and understand your female and male nature. This will in turn help you to better understand your partner's female and male nature, the "Yin and Yang☯" of him and her. Man and woman are no different; they have their dualities like everything else in nature. In book II of I Ching the two underlying principles are described in the following words:

> *Heaven is high, the earth is low;*
> *thus the Creative and Receptive are determined.*
> *In correspondence with this difference between low and high,*
> *inferior and superior places are established.*
> *Movement and rest have their definite laws;*
> *according to these,*
> *firm and yielding lines are differentiated.*
> *Events follow definite trends,*
> *each according to its nature.*
> *Things are distinguished from one another in definite classes.*
> *In this way good fortune and misfortune come about.*
> *In the heavens phenomena take form;*
> *on earth shapes take form.*
> *In this way change and transformation become manifest.*

OPPOSITE SEX FRIENDSHIP

I think it is important for me to discuss under relationship [we-lationship] marital partners having friends of the opposite sex. Opposite-sex friendships can work but can be very tricky and more importantly, can be a direct threat to the relationship you have with your spouse. For most couples the fear does not come from the friendship, but from keeping the friendship platonic, which can be very difficult.

In these types of friendships, 90 percent of the time one of the individuals has experienced romantic feelings for his/her friend. Sometimes in these relationships, the couples talk about their friendship with the opposite sex and other times it is not discussed. However, it should be openly discussed in the marriage, whereby each partner gives the other assurance that it is platonic. By limiting your friendships with the opposite sex, once you are married, does not allow the riches and perspective that a partner could gain from having a friend of the opposite sex. When couples have an understanding and foresight as to what the boundaries should be, then it is possible to have friends of the opposite sex and keep your marriage strong and healthy. The following are some don'ts and do's for opposite-sex friendships:

DON'TS

- No secrets, all parties should know each other and the friend of the opposite sex should know and respect the fact that the couple is married.
- The amount of time spent with the friend should never supersede the time spent with your spouse, unless there is a dire emergency.
- Never make an agreement with the friend that cannot be changed. The agreement should always be negotiable, for instance, if the agreement with your friend is not acceptable to your spouse, it should be modified or cancelled.
- Never make your spouse feel that he or she is not the most important person to you; always respect the sensitivity of your spouse feelings.
- Never put your friend's needs before your spouse. Keep your spouse as your number-one priority and then any mystery surrounding the friendship diminishes. Also, your spouse will more likely view the friend as a person and not just a fantasy. This will keep it from being non-

threatening to the relationship [welationship].

<u>*DO'S*</u>

- To ensure comfort and trust, there needs to be a high level of maturity and self-esteem with all persons involved. Do not think your spouse will get it through osmosis; you must thoroughly communicate this to your spouse and really talk about everyone's concerns and fears.

- Establish ground rules at the beginning of an opposite-sex friendship, such as what is okay and what is not. For example, is it okay for the friend to get together when the spouse is out of town? How much time is spent with the friend on a monthly basis? What do the friends do when they are together; is dancing okay, is having dinner okay? These are just a few ground rules, each marital couple should come up with their own individual concerns and questions to consider and mutual agree on them.

- All parties need to be in agreement that it is okay for the friendship to even exist. Neither spouse's opinion should be left out of the process.

- The spouse with the opposite sex friend needs to have strong clear personal boundaries and open communication with their spouse and their friend. Further, The spouse with the friend needs to be up front at all times with their spouse, letting him or her know when they are seeing their friend.

- If one spouse ever feels uncomfortable with the arrangement, he or she should be able to speak up at any time without an argument ensuing. Their feelings and concerns must be considered and taken very seriously, in order to deal with them appropriately.

In theory, most spouses want their partners to be happy and to have friends of the opposite sex. However, in reality, this can only comfortably happen by following the above stated ground rules. In most instances, the main issues surrounding these friendships are usually jealously and physical intimacy. If you can talk about your friend freely with your spouse and make him or her a real person, then it is less likelihood of these types of problems occurring. It is important to always keep the lines of communication open at all times with everyone involved. Furthermore, be honest with yourself about your ability to have good boundaries and clarity about what is appropriate in a friendship and your marriage. Bear in mind there are differences in the way you interact with your spouse than with your friend. As long as everything is out in the open and having clear defined ground rules a friendship with the opposite sex could be possible. However, if you notice the friendship moving into a more intimacy direction and both of you become attractive to each other, then you must back off and call it off early on.

Usually, cheating is not a spur of the moment thing, even more so if you are really into your spouse. When you miss your spouse you do not look for away to hurt or deceive them. However, if that opposite-sex friend is available it makes cheating much easier, especially if the other spouse at home becomes boring and the marriage is no longer fun. Who knows the answer to the long-standing question as to, are cheaters born cheaters or do certain situations cause people to cheat? The answer, probably a little bit of both; the following are situations that might give some reasons as to why a spouse cheat:

1. _Bored_ – This is possible the most common reason that a spouse might cheat. It can be hard to keep that lovable edge throughout the marriage. Things can start off grand and then before you know it things level off and the interest is lost. Then you meet someone else that generates some excitement in your life and before you realize it, a new relationship jumps off.

2. *Dependence* – The cheater seems to like independent behavior, it could be interpreted as doing what you want, when you want. On the other hand, it can be strongly argue that cheating is a dependent behavior. A cheater is dependent, in that he or she is not strong enough to break up with their spouse in order to get with the new person.

3. *Confusion* – Letting life or a particular situation get to you and you become confused in making sound judgment. This becomes a perfect storm for confusion to get in your head and you start cheating.

4. *Forgiveness* – When you forgive a cheater, it means you are putting up with it and starts a vicious cycle. The spouse who cheated may lose respect for the other spouse and might continue to cheat, because they know they can get away with it, and you will continue to take them back. The exception to this would be if both partners were willing to go to a professional counselor and seek help for their problem(s).

5. *Nurturing* – If you are being mistreated, your first instinct is to get away from him or her. However, it is not always that simple, because maybe sometimes you are raising children together. When you feel trapped in a bad relationship, it is only natural that you will run to the open arms of a person who treats you well.

6. *Revenge* – This one is quite simple, one spouse wants to get revenge on the other one for cheating (the old eye for an eye concept). The mind-set, I will cheat on him or her if he or she cheats on me. It is done to only get back at the cheater. Know that this is not healthy emotionally for either spouse.

7. *Confirmation of Attractiveness* – When you have been

married for several years or your spouse is taking you for granted, then you begin to wonder if you are still attractive. Perhaps, when you were out on the dating circuit you felt more attractive then you do since you have gotten married.

8. _For The Thrill of it_ – Some people enjoy the thrill of cheating; running around secretly; risk getting caught and the creating thrilling moments with a forbidden romance.

The following are signs most cheaters exhibit:

- Starting to act differently than the way he/she used too.
- Starting to avoid you by coming home much later, making excuses to get out of the house and/or going away with out you on the weekends.
- Having less or no sex, whereas he/she used to be very romantic and feel more like making love, but now it just feels like plain old having sex.
- Have become very private by keeping their cell phone hidden, stop checking e-mails in front of you and start receiving bills at the office.

If you notice any of these signs do not hesitate to discuss them with your spouse. Tell him/her that things feel different than they used to and you would like an explanation as to why. Do not turn a blind eye on your relationship if things are bad, getting bad or just feel strange, do something about it. In other words you should address them early on while they are small. Maintain a strong relationship [welationship] by keeping an open communication is one of the best things you can do to ensure fidelity on both spouses part.

With some spouses, cheating becomes a way of life and they tend to rationalize and justify it by making excuses and blaming their partner. The cheating spouse feels if their partner has not talked about exclusivity, then it is all right to see other people even though their

spouse may not. I am reminded of a counseling session I had with a
young married couple on cheating. One spouse said to the cheating
spouse, "You not only cheated on me, you cheated on yourself; you
not only disrespected me, you disrespected yourself; you not only deceived me, you deceived yourself; and you not only hurt me emotionally, you hurt yourself, as well as our children." The spouse added,
"Our entire family is suffering as a result of your thoughtless behavior." During the counseling session, I thought about what was said and
realized it was a very powerful statement. The tragedy of the story was
not only embarrassing to the cheating spouse, but to the other spouse
and the family members as well. So think of the consequences that
could possible result before you embark upon a cheating escapade.
You could be the grand loser. Here are some profound reminders to
help you solidify your relationship [welationship] with your spouse:

1. *Communication* – Be a good communicator by talking
    openly and truthfully with your spouse regarding any
    and all family concerns. In theory, all behavior is a form
    of communication, whether or not we speak or make eye
    contact at all, our behaviors send messages and hence
    communicate something. Therefore, we must be sensi-
    tive as to how we are sending messages to our spouse,
    in that it might be misread. Good communication helps
    to improve the relationship and turn it into a welation-
    ship and keep both spouses together and connected. In
    order to be a communicator, it requires having good ac-
    tive listening skills. How well you listen has a major
    impact on the quality of your relationship [welationship]
    with your spouse; because, we listen to obtain informa-
    tion, to understand, to learn and for enjoyment. You can
    improve your relationship [welationship] tremendously
    by becoming a better listener, because when you listen
    you hear the whole message. The best way to become a

better listener is to practice what is called, "active listen-ing." This is where you make a conscious effort to hear not only words that your spouse is saying but, more im-portantly, to try and understand the total message being conveyed.

2. *Respect* – giving each other respect has a lot to do with how you view, relate and admire each other in your rela-tionship [welationship]. Respecting each other's needs, opinions and space will improve your relationship [we-lationship] on an even greater level.

3. *Trust* – having trust in your relationship [welationship] is the primary building block that ultimately keeps a couple together. When there is trust, a couple can over-come any conflict or obstacle that may arise.

4. *Commitment* – finding common ground and committing to each other creates a strong bond that cannot be bro-ken. Proving your commitment to each other on a daily basis will strengthen and improve your relationship [we-lationship].

5. *Support* – having a spouse that supports you, even when no one else does, is the greatest form of devotion. Sup-port comes from within. Building on support improves the mental, as well as the physical part of a good rela-tionship [welationship]. Always be your spouse-leading cheerleader.

6. *Stability* – there is no greater foundation for improving a relationship [welationship] than stability. Stability creates an atmosphere of structure, which improves the very existence of a great relationship [welationship].

7. *Self Confidence* – spouses must have self-confidence as to their individual roles in the relationship [welation-ship]. Having high self-esteem and self-confidence im-

proves the marriage and guides it through a healthy and satisfying existence.

PARENTING

Among the many reasons for getting married, procreation ranks at the very top of the list. It is said, "The birth of a baby is God's way of saying, the world must continue to exist." However, raising children to be productive citizens can be a major undertaking, in that it takes time, effort, energy, and money, as well as the responsibilities and concerns that go along with it. Like with married couples, communication is a direr must with children, however, to get them to talk sometime becomes a chore. It has been reported that only 30 percent of middle and high school-aged students surveyed have a positive family communication with their parents. It appears that positive family communication is more common with younger children than older teenagers. It is extremely important to have the positive conversation about the important things in life, such as alcohol, drugs and sexual activity with your children. The following are some ideas you can utilize daily with your children:

Stay Connected

- Talk with your children every day; once your children learn that they can trust you with the "little stuff," they will trust you with the "big stuff." Just remember you are their parents and not their friend and also let them know that you have their best interest at heart.
- Create times for talking, for instance require all family members to have the evening meals together. Turn off the radio while driving and have a positive conversation, also turn off the television and spend some quality time together.
- Be approachable, if children think they will get a

lecture or be judged every time they bring up an idea or a personal problem, they will be hesitant to communicate. Try to listen without judging and ask questions without accusing. Show that you under- stand what children are feeling by sharing similar experiences.

- Take your children concerns seriously, sometimes it is easy to dismiss their concerns or worries because, from an adult perspective it does not seem impor- tant. However, it is important to them and you as a parent should not take them lightly, laugh it off or tease them about it. It is important to your children that you listen and show interest in what they are saying. Then they will not be hesitant to come to you about other things, which you will be glad they did because of their importance.

- Do not wait for an important conversation to talk with your children, find time to talk with them ev- eryday about both trivial and important issues. When you have these conversation really listen to what your children have to say.

- Be patient, your children may be tired or upset, sometimes they are not ready to talk. Give and re- spect your children space, but do not let it become an excuse to avoid conversation. There will be times when you and your children will say things that you regret. Other times you will miss an opportunity to have a positive conversation with them. Just relax, this is perfectly normal. Despite the fact that you may be having a hard time talking, remember to al- ways start a new conversation, even a simple one, that can help get you back on track.

- Listen for more than just words, in terms of what your children are saying. It may show through their tone or other actions. Listen very carefully and try to understand the feeling behind the words, not just the words themselves.

- Think through the tough conversations, sometimes you need to have difficult conversations, then ask yourself: what should I say? What can I do to make it go well? What do they need from me, etc.?

- Be creative with your children, have a conversation when you are hiking in the mountains, shooting basketball or working on a project. Doing things that both of you enjoy doing, this may be the best way to get a conversation started.

- Communicate without talking, there are several ways to communicate to children that you care without uttering a word such as, leaving a caring note, send a friendly e-mail, or set by their bed side and give them a backrub, etc.

- Give your children time, sometime they need space to work through things and figure out who they are. Give them time and space, but let them know you are always there for them and you are ready and willing to listen. Frequently say the three most powerful words in any language to them, *"I LOVE YOU."*

As a parent the above suggestions should help to establish a good relationship with your children whereby, you are able to positively communicate with them on any topic.

Communicating with your children also includes disciplining them. The Biblical Scripture in *The Living Bible*, Proverbs 22: 6, Solomon states, "Teach a child to choose the right path, and when he is older he will remain upon it." Learning how to discipline your children is an important skill that all parents need to learn. Discipline is not the same as punishment. Discipline has to do more with teaching your children right from wrong such as, how to respect the rights of others; what behaviors are acceptable and which are not; helping to set goals to develop your children to feel secure and loved; to be self-confident; self-disciplined; teach them how to control their impulses; and how not to get overly frustrated with the normal stresses of everyday life. If you are experiencing difficulty in disciplining your children, it is important to remember that you may not be doing anything wrong, so do not beat up on yourself. All children are different and have different temperaments and developmental levels and a style of discipline that may work with one child may not work with another child. It is important to understand that how you behave when disciplining your children will help to determine how your children are going to behave or misbehave in the future. If you give in after your children repeatedly argues with you, becomes violent or have a temper tantrum, then they will learn to repeat this type of behavior because they know you may eventually give in (even if it is only once in awhile that you do give in). If you are firm, stern and consistent then your children will learn it does not pay to fight doing what they are eventually going to have to do anyway. However, some children will feel like they won if they put off doing something that they did not want to do for even a few minutes. As the parents, you must be consistent in your methods of discipline and how you punish your children. This applies to all child-care givers. It is normal for children to test their limits and if you are inconsistent in what these limits are then you will be encouraging more misbehavior. Some important reminders about discipline:

- Stay calm and do not get carried away when your children misbehave. Avoid yelling and screaming, since this can teach your children that it is all right to lose self-control if you do not get your way. Plus it can make them nervous, jittery and/or uneasy. As a parent, if you feel things are escalating too much, then take a break until you can regain your composure. If it does not work the first time, step back and take a deep breath and try it again. Children love to push their parents to the limits; it is just what growing up is all about.

- Avoid criticizing your children too much, make sure they understand that it is the misbehavior that you are unhappy with and not them that you will always love them.

- Avoid giving your children too much praise; you do not need to be continuously praising them, especially for routine activities. It makes your comments less effective when they really do something outstanding.

- Do not always focus on the negativity all the time, especially when you are offering positive reinforcement. It is much better to say, "I like that you put all of your clothes away," instead of saying, "I like that, for once, you finally got around to putting your clothes away without my asking."

- At all cost avoid physical punishment. Spanking has never been shown to be more effective than other forms of punishment and will make your children more aggressive, violent and angry; and in some instances fearful of you as their parents. So never raise your hand or use foul language when you are discipline your children. Violence and bad language just make the situation turn into something un-called-for. Violence has never cause anything but more violence. Patience, persistence and love are all you need to properly discipline your children.

- Remember to give rewards and praises for good behavior. However, understand the difference between rewards and bribes. A reward is something your children receive after he or she has done something nice, while a bribe is given beforehand to try to motivate the child to do what you want done. Bribes should be avoided.

- Be a good role model for your children. Always model good positive behavior in your children presence through your actions, as well as the words you speak. Most importantly, always provide your children with a safe environment in which they can feel secure and well loved.

One of the most rewarding experience parents can receive in life is raising well polite, good and healthy productive children. After all, they are our best and brightest, as well as our future leaders.

There are a growing number of women who are putting off marriage and childbearing to pursue their professional careers. College attendance among women has doubled; one out of five women obtained some college education in the mid 60's compared to two out of five in the early 80's. Female students constituted over half of the student body at two-year colleges, as well as about half of the student body at four-year colleges/universities. In recent decades, the percentage of young women obtaining advanced degrees and pursuing a professional career has increase dramatically to the detriment of a decline in marriages. The ever-increasing opportunities for women to work outside their homes have made them less economically dependent on their husbands. Due to the stiff competition in the workplace to retain a job, the desire to pursue careers and attain promotions through organization structure can delay marriage. As a result, the marriage institution seems to be undergoing a rebellious and dramatic shift with more women entering the workplace. The trend appears to be toward people not wanting to commit for the long term but are deciding just to live together. Neither young men nor young women regard delaying marriage as a negative thing. However, research shows this is the first generation of women who have had equal opportunities to men in education and career; which has caused a decrease in marriage and having children. According to census data, women with higher incomes have the highest childless rates.

On the other hand, about 33 percent of all births were attributed to unmarried women. I am walking a tightrope here discussing this subject, but it is a walk too vital not to take. Just know my intent is not to degrade, belittle, judge or be critical of anyone, but only to help by sharing some words of wisdom and/or provoke some sensible thought. It is my personal belief that it is the ultimate responsibility of a woman to prevent childbirth if she knows the participating male is vehemently opposed to having a child. The man should not be criticized and/or castigated for not wanting her to birth his child. A woman should never, never ever allows a man to violate her body, which I refer to as her "temple." Further she should not allow any man to enter her temple that she deems not worthy; it should be her decision, only exception, if she raped. However, this by no way absorbs males of their personal responsibilities. I must hastily add that several women have voice this same understanding to me, so I am not out here on an island by myself. When I interviewed several women about this subject, they tell me there are multiple reasons why this is such a frequent occurrence of women with the following not being the least:

- The number one reason is to get marry. It is said, in general, "That women are the winners of marriage."
- To try and get the man to fall in love with them.
- The baby will be the connection to keep them together, (the baby daddy syndrome) a life long connection.
- To acquire child support, as well as self-support (fi-

nancial stability).

- Control and manipulation – telling the man his child needs "this and that."

There is another burning issue with women whether or not womanhood can co-exist without motherhood. Womanhood holds a distinct place in our universal life experience. Women are not meant merely to be men's opposite or to just bear children; they are meant to be and express themselves. They are distinctive beings with their own place in the world to fulfill and to complete their own life's work. Unequivocally, they are not what society has portrayed them to be. Male poets, painters, sculptors and novelists, all have endeavored to portray the ideal woman as she appeared to them or as it seemed to them she should be. Yet it would hardly be safe for women to model upon these portrayals; it is imperative that women discover themselves and present themselves in the way they want to be portrayed. When we look about us for the form of self-expression that belongs distinctively to women, we find that it is motherhood that belongs to her alone. She is the mother of the race and in this function we shall find embodied in her, supreme power. However, this does not mean that every woman wants to be or necessarily intended to be a physical mother. Womanhood springs from her individuality. To realize this, she must first of all find herself. It is important that she takes time to think about herself and what she was intended to be. She must know her shortcomings and set herself resolutely to work to master her weaknesses. Also, she must learn to glory in her womanly nature, which she possesses like no other, and through this make the most of what lay deeply hidden within her. This must be her forever aim. The obligation rests upon her to arouse herself and in the full consciousness of her strength to be able to rise to heights of world service such has never known before. The perfect woman has never been revealed. However, the woman who is well developed on all sides of her nature physically, mentally, emotionally and spiritually may be looked upon as having attained a degree of perfection. So it is my conclusion that there should be no further arguments, without question, that womanhood and motherhood can definite co-exist.

TOXIC FAMILY MEMBERS

Absent of working hard at it, it could be an uphill battle to maintain a meaningful relationship [welationship] with your spouse. However, it can be even worse to have a meaningful and/or worthwhile relationship with family members. Some family members can be very contemptuous and at worse, very toxic in their behavior and actions toward you. Family members consist of parents, children, siblings, aunts, uncle, grandparents, cousins and in-laws. A fact of life: we are not born loners; we all want and need good family relationships with other family members in order to be happy, connected and successful in life. Another fact of life: family relationships are tough. Some family members always want something from you when you are not willing or able to accommodate them. This can cause deep emotional hurt. Third fact of life: family relationships are tougher to maintain than with your spouse. Think about it, you are very close to your family members; you probably lived in the same house together with them for many years. They know you very well, your quirks, your moods and most of all, how and when to push your buttons. Family members know how to get you to react to their criticism and/ or rejection in a way other people would not necessary react. I call this "toxic family relationship behavior." When you are dealing with toxic family members' behavior in your life, it can drag you down, make you feel angry, make you feel worn out, deflated, belittled, ridiculed and/or confused. Toxic family members cause undue stress, anxiety and even depression, especially during holidays and on special occasions, which should be the time to be about family, love and togetherness. Most of us could write a long laundry list of names of family members who make us feel miserable when they are around us.

They spew their unhealthy negative attitudes, have bad behaviors and are constantly gossiping, create much confusion and discontentment. Some family members have the tendency and ridiculous ability to be two-faced in their dealing with other family members. Usually, toxic family members' behaviors are extremely negative, miserable, whiny, jealous, inconsiderate, financially irresponsible, manipulative, narcissistic, selfish, disrespectful, gossipmongers, mentally and emotionally abusive bullies who have no boundaries. I probably left out some adjectives to describe some toxic family members, so you can create your own list. According to mental health specialists and psychologists, toxic family members are "highly insecure individuals who only feel better about themselves if they make others feel worse. They cause over 50% of all negative communication, stress in other family members and health problem such as: headaches, stomach pain and digestive problems, due to the negative baggage brought on by their low self-esteem." Toxic family members are this way because they can and often get away with it and it works well for them. If it did not work for them, they would not continue to do it. If it is not properly dealt with, toxic family members will do the following:

- Rob you of your dignity
- Destroy your self-confidence
- Increase your stress levels
- Cause health problems
- Destroy your morale
- Destroy family relationships
- Foster negativity
- Decrease productivity
- Get you fired from your job
- Drive you to bankruptcy, and much more

The best way to deal with toxic family members is to recognize that they have personal issues within themselves and their toxicity has everything to do with them and nothing to do with you. In our life experiences, everyone has to take personal responsibility for his or her own choices, attitudes, actions, inactions and behaviors however; toxic family members do not do this. You become their personal target. They will habitually turn things around and manipulate the situation and/or you to the point where you are made to feel bad, guilty, and even make you feel as though you are at fault and responsible for their problems. At times, you can even begin to feel like you are going crazy or losing your mind, wondering if you have become a victim of their desperate attempt of trying to manipulate and control you. Once you recognize the toxic behaviors that are engulfing your life and health, it allows you to take your power back and be in control of your life experience. There becomes a time that you must realize that you cannot help them and that you should not allow them to pull you down in their mess.

For additional information concerning courtship and marriage, I suggest you read the book I wrote titled, *Universal Cosmic Messages For Courtship And Marriage.*

My following *Wardisms* are to share some additional information on the subject, "relationship /WELATIONSHIP:"

If we were to replace the word relationship
with the word welationship, we might stay
rather than stray and run away.

W

A single woman dating a married man has
little chance of future wedding plans.

W

In your relationship/welationship,
you should never smash, bash, trash,
say or do anything ill will against
your mate, it will cause lots of hate.

W

When your relationship/welationship
is in doubt, it might be worth making up
before you bow out and break up.

W

Do not hate your mate, try and reduce
the divorce rate by having a happier fate.

W

Love serves no other intent, purpose or
desire than to fulfill its destiny to love.

W

Above all, love is the essence of our cause.

W

Always be firm like a brick wall,
stand tall and never let your
relationship/welationship fall apart.

W

I am the master of my fate, I need not
hate or be late to meet my soul mate.

W

A good date with your mate might make
you stay and keep you from running away.

W

When you teach your child the right way to
live, he or she will not stray along the way.

W

Love is the essence of all humankind, so
always keep this in mind and you will be
fine all the time and never left behind.

W

Never be late on your date and take
some silly bate that will cause you to
hate and lose your mate.

W

A wife's tongue can be sharp as a knife,
so keep strife out of your married life.

W

If you choose the right spouse he or she
will always be twice as nice in your house.

W

If you treat your spouse nice and kind, you
will always have peace of mind.

W

When there is uncontrollable confusion by one mate
and no harmony in your house, you might need to
change your spouse.

W

A person in a relationship/welationship filled
with heat has no reason to sneak or cheat.

W

Open your mouth and say, *"I Love You,"* the three
most powerful words you can say, which may keep
your relationship/welationship from going south
(downhill).

W

I am your husband, you are my wife, with our
beautiful children let's live a wonderful happy life
with riches abundantly.

W

Do not hate your mate just participate so everything
will be lovely and great, even
when you are late for a date.

W

Make your relationship/welationship
work for you and do not work against its
love, peace, joy, kindness and happiness.

When you promote peace, love, joy and
happiness in your house, you will not
experience any problems with your spouse.

Day or night, in or out, right or wrong share
your love so you will not be alone.

You may serve them rice and treat them
nice, but some people may take your kindness for
weakness and treat you like mice, so think twice and
give up any immoral vices you might have, because
it might keep your relationship/welationship from
melting like ice.

In summation, I have written a lot concerning this topic, but if we can simply remember, having a good relationship/welationship starts with a foundation based on these profound reminders: communication, respect, trust, commitment, support, stability, self-confidence and respecting each other's space. Never confuse the wedding with the marriage and equally important is to never confuse the first argument with the honeymoon. Your foundation must be strong and stable to the point of not allowing any outside forces to interrupt its sanctity; these include friends, family members and/or anything tangible or intangible. However, there will be times when your relationship/welationship will be put to the grand old test to find out how strong it really is. If both partners are able to stand tall and willingly to face whatever the problem(s) maybe together and adhere to some of the suggestions given above, then together your relationship/welationship

will survive. Then you will know you have a true **WELATIONSHIP.**
Remember, a loving relationship [welationship] must be based upon togetherness, connectedness, inseparability and interdependence. It must have love as it core motivator, as well as peace, joy and happiness. You must always seek to see the good in your spouse and not the negative. Know that your relationship [welationship] becomes what you want it to become, a lasting one will live in perpetuity on love, peace, joy and happiness. Remember, know and accept the fact that love and hate cannot coexist in the same place.

Once again, I strongly advise and invite you to read my book entitled, *Universal Cosmic Messages For Courtship And Marriage*, which will give you a greater and more in depth understanding on this topic, "RELATIONSHIP."

"LOVE YE ONE ANOTHER"
And
BE PEACEFULLY HAPPY!

4
DEATH

This is a subject that is not written or talked about to the degree that I think it should. I do not know whether it is because we fear its morbidity; we have a lack of command to intelligently discuss it or we think we will avoid its inevitability; so forth and so on. Personally, I believe death/transition should be discussed in homes with family members, in the various religious structures with their spiritual leaders and elsewhere, so people may lose their fears and better understand that we all have to face this ineluctability.

The word "death" in the Aramaic language, the oldest Biblical language in the world means: "to be present somewhere else." It does not mean annihilation, nor does it means to cease to exist. We must understand life before we can understand that death is not final, but always a new beginning. I like to think of death as a transitional process from one place in space in time to another place in space in time. We must get rid of the fear and the unpleasant thoughts we have about death; we should view life and death as an interchange between rest and action. They are an eternal continuity of repeated interchanges with each other, because life could not live without death and death could not die without life. Walter Russell said in his book titled, *The Message Of The Divine Iliad Volume 1:*

> If life interchanges with death, that means that life is giving itself to death and death to life. In other words, life and

death continually void each other. Life integrates and death disintegrates. Each becomes the other alternately. Each is one-half of a cycle. Cycles cannot continue indefinitely, but they must be forever repeated sequentially.

We are born from the seed of life and the seed of death is also born within us. In other words, life gives birth to death and death gives birth to life with one being in the womb and the other in tomb. Each day our bodies die while we are constantly renewing it with nourishment, which is a constant renewal and a repair process. The part of our bodies that died has to be renewed with living tissue.

Some people believe death is the permanent termination of life. However, the effect of physical death on any possible mind or soul remains an open question yet to be answered. Religions, almost without exception, maintain faith in either some kind of afterlife or reincarnation. The following explains the various religious views on death:

- **Christianity**

  For Christians who are guided by the Holy Bible, the reality of death is acknowledged as part of the current human condition, affected by sin, i.e.: Genesis 2: 17, "But of the tree of knowledge of good and evil, thou shalt not eat of it: for in the day that thou eatest thereof thou shall surely die." Romans 5: 12, "Wherefore, as by one man sin entered into the world, and death by sin; and so death passed upon all men, for that all have sinned." Ecclesiastes 3: 2, there is "A time to be born, and a time to die; a time to plant, and a time to puck up that which is planted." Christians further believe eternal life is a gift that is granted to all who accept salvation through Jesus Christ. Also, faithful Christians await the second coming of Jesus for complete realization of their immortality (John 3: 36; Romans 6: 23; 1 Corinthians 15: 51-

54). [The aforementioned scriptures are quotes from the *King James Version.*] While waiting for Jesus to come again, Christians may be called upon to care for the dying and to personally face their own death.

- ## Islam

When death approaches, the close family and friends try to support and comfort the dying person through supplication as well as remembrance of Allah and His will. They help the dying person to iterate his commitment to unity of God. Upon death, the eyelids are to be closed, the body should be covered, and preparation for burial takes place soon as possible. The whole body is washed and wrapped in a shroud. Muslims gather to perform a pray for the dead. The body is to be buried soon after the prayer. The wrapped body is to be laid directly at the bottom of the dug grave. The body is to be laid on its right side facing the direction of Makkah (the holy place were Muslims perform pilgrimage). A ceiling is attached to the grave and then covered with dirt. The grave is to be marked by raising its top level of dirt above surrounding grounds. A stone may be used to mark its location, but no writings are allowed. Buildings or other forms of structures are not allowed on top of the grave. The family of the dead has a responsibility to fulfill any debts of the deceased as soon as possible. Also, they have the commitment to maintain contacts and courteous relationships with close relatives and close friends. They frequently pray and supplicate for the deceased. Charity, fasting, prayer and pilgrimage is often performed on behalf of the dead. Visiting the graves is recommended for the living to remember death and the Day of Judgment.

- ### Hinduism

Hinduism believes in the rebirth and reincarnation of souls. Death is therefore not a great calamity, not an end at all, but a natural process in the existence of soul as a separate entity, by which it reassembles its resources, adjusts its course and returns again to the earth to continue its journey. In Hinduism death is a temporary cessation of physical activity, a necessary means of recycling the resources and energy and an opportunity for the soul along with some residual consciousness leaves the body through an opening in the head and goes to another world and returns again after spending some time there. What happens after the soul leaves the body and before it reincarnates again is a great mystery. The Bhagavad-Gita describes two paths along which souls travel after death. One is the path of the sun, also known as the bright path and the other is the path of the moon, also known as the dark path. When a soul travels along the path of the sun, it never return again, those that travel along the path of the moon return again. What happens to a soul after death of a mortal being on earth depends upon many factors. Some of which are his previous deeds, his state of mind at the time of death, the time he dies, the activities of his children, that is whether they performed the funeral rites in the prescribed manner and satisfied the scriptural injunctions. Hinduism believes in the existence of not one hell and one heaven but in the existence of many sun filled worlds and many dark and demonic worlds. Vaikunth is the world of Vishnu, Kailash is the world of Siva and Brahmalok is the world of Brahman. Indralok is the standard heaven to which those who please the gods through their activities upon the earth go. The standard hell is Yamalok, which is also ruled by a god called Lord Yama, who is also the ruler of the southern quarter. In the ultimate sense, the purpose of these worlds is neither to punish or reward the souls, but to remind them of the true purpose of their existence. After death, Hindus are not buried, but cremated. The idea is that the human personality is made up of five elements of which four belong to the body and come from the world, namely fire, earth, water and air while the fifth the ether (fine matter) belongs to the domain of the subtle body and comes from the higher words. By cremating the body, the elements are rightfully returned to their respective spheres, while the subtle body along with the soul returns to the worlds beyond for the continuation of its afterlife. A lot of rituals are associated with the cremation ceremony. When a person dies, the body is given a final bath, carried on a wooden stretcher by his kith and kin and cremated on the community cremation grounds generally by the eldest son. This is followed by some rituals in which the sons make offering of food to the departed soul under the supervision of a priest. Generally a function is organized on the fifteen-day and guests are invited for a meal. Hindus who have lost an important relation in their families do not celebrate functions and festivals for a specific period of time as a mark of respect. While cremation is the standard procedure, Hindus consider it very suspicious if a dead body is immersed in the Ganges or cremated on its banks since the river is considered very sacred.

- **Buddhism**

From its inception, Buddhism has stressed the importance of death, since awareness of death is what prompted the Buddha to perceive the ultimate futility of worldly concerns and pleasures. Realizing that death is inevitable for a person who is caught up in worldly pleasures and attitudes; he/she resolved to renounce the world and devote their time to finding a solution to this most basic of existential dilemmas. A Buddhist looks at death as a breaking apart of the material of which we are composed. However Buddhism does not look at death as a continuation of the soul but as an awakening. Dying and being reborn has been compared by some Buddhist as a candle flame. When the flame of one lit candle is touched to the wick of an unlighted candle, the light passes from one candle to another. The actual flame of the first candle does not pass over but is responsible for lighting the second candle. When preparing for death Buddhist generally agree that a person's state of mind while dying is of great importance. While dying the person can be surrounded by friends, family and monks who recite Buddhists scriptures and mantras to help the person achieve a peaceful state of mind. Buddhism asserts that all being live beyond the various fluctuation of this life. Death is merely a passage to rebirth in another realm such as the human world, a pure land or the flowering of the ultimate nature of the mind. In Buddhism, death is not the end of life, it is merely the end of this body we inhabit in this life, but our spirit will still remain and seek out through the need of attachment to a new body and a new life. Where they will be born is a result of the past and the accumulation of positive and negative action, and the resultant of karma (cause and effect) is a result of ones past actions.

- **Zoroastrianism**

  The Parsees (Zoroastrians) do not cremate, bury or submerge their dead in water because they consider the dead to be impure, and their Zoroastrian faith does not permit them to defile any of the elements with them. This desert ritual, which originated along with their faith in Persia more than 3,000 years ago and regards death not as the work of God but of the devil, dictates that the dead be left to vultures on hilltops. It is common for Parsees to travel long distances to bring their dead to Mumbai towers (India) because prayers for the dead can only be said for those who have passed through its gates. Dead Parsees are carried on a bier to a ceremonial gate near the five Towers of Silence, where relatives hand them to pallbearers, the only people allowed inside. The black stone towers, about 36 meters high, are like three-tiered, open-air arenas where the men are placed in the outer circle, women in the middle and children in the innermost for the vultures to feed on. But with an average of three Parsees dying every day, the handful of vultures at the towers are overfed. Experts' say about 100-120 birds would be needed to deal with the daily intake bodies. The Zoroastrians, or Parsees, have installed solar reflectors in their Towers of Silence in Mumbai to help dispose of their dead after a decline in the number of vultures that scavenge their corpses in keeping with tradition.

- **Judaism**

  Judaism has stressed the natural fact of death and its role in giving life meaning. The fear of death, concern about the fate of our own soul and those of our loved ones, ethical concerns that some people die unfairly, all these and many other issues are discussed in Jewish literature. Since God is seen as ultimately just, the seeming injustice on earth has propelled many traditional Jewish thinkers into seeing the afterlife as a way to reflect the ultimate justice of human existence. Traditional thinkers considered how individuals would be rewarded or punished after their deaths. There are a few rare descriptions of life after death. Traditionalists gave the name Gehenna to the place where souls were punished. Many Jewish thinkers noted that since God is filled with mercy and love, punishment is not to be considered to be eternal. There are, similarly, many varying conceptions of paradise; such as that paradise is the place where we finally understand the true concept of God. It is also possible that there is no separate Heaven and Hell, only lesser or greater distance from God after death. Judaism does not believe people who are Gentiles will automatically go to Hell or that Jews will automatically go to Heaven on their basis of their belonging to the faith. Rather, individual ethical behavior is what is most important.

It is clear, predicated on the above, that there are many different kind of beliefs and ways people of their given religion deal with death/transition.

There are some common sense things one can do to prepare for their transition, in order to make it less stressful and emotional painless for their loved ones. There are many types of legal documents that can help you plan how you want your affairs handled when you make your transition. Many of these documents sound alike and that they would achieve the same results, not necessary the case, make sure you are using the documents you want. State laws vary, so find out about the rules, requirements and forms applicable to your State. Wills and trusts allow you to name the person(s) to whom you want to receive your money and property after your death.

- A living will gives you a say in your health care if you are too sick to make your wishes known. In a living will, you can say what kind of care you do or do not want. This will make it easier for family members to make tough decisions for you when you are unable to do so yourself.

- There are different types of powers of attorney. A power of attorney is a written document in which you appoint someone else to act for you, as your legal agent. Everyone should consider having a power of attorney, it can be quite important to your personal well-being. It allows you to pick someone you trust, while still being of sound mind, to handle your affairs if you are unable to do so yourself. Also, it gives you peace of mind, knowing that in an emergency someone you choose will have the authority to act on your behalf. Absent of not having a power of attorney and you were suddenly incapacitated could cost your family members great expense and can be time-consuming for the court to appoint a guardian or conservator. Types of power of attorney: (1) A conventional power of attorney begins when you sign it and continues until you become mentally incapacitated. (2) A durable power of attorney also begins when you sign it, but it stays in effect for your lifetime, unless you cancel it. If it is for health care decisions, make sure the person you name is willing to make decisions for you. (3) A springing power of attorney begins when a specific event happens such as, when you become incapacitated. This document must be carefully drafted to avoid any difficulty in determining exactly when the "Springing" event happens. All powers of attorney come to an end at your death; your agent will have no power to make any decisions after you make your transition. It is imperative that you seek legal consultation before deciding on the power of attorney that would best meet your needs, as well as all the above-mentioned legal documents.

The following are things you can do for yourself:

1. *A will* – If you do not have a will, get one. It is important to update your will periodically.

2. *Make sure all of your assets are titled correctly* – For example, a bank account held by two people as "joints tenants" transfers differently than if it were jointly owned with "right of survivorship."

3. *Make sure contractual beneficiary designations are current* – Such as, life insurance, annuities, IRAs and retirement plans can all be transferred contractually by naming a beneficiary. It is important to keep these beneficiary designations updated.

4. *Make sure you have a financial power of attorney* – A financial power of attorney simply empowers a trusted individual to manage your financial affairs should you become incapacitated, it ceases upon your recovery or transition.

5. *Frequently evaluate your life insurance needs, purchase additional coverage if necessary* – For instance, if you have married, taken on a mortgage or had additional children, it may be necessary for you to increase your insurance coverage. Remember that life insurance is cheaper while you are young.

6. *Make a list of all-important persons to contact* – This list should contain the names, home addresses, e-mail addresses, and telephone numbers of all-important contacts. This list should include, but not limited to your

banker, broker, insurance agent, attorney, accountant, financial advisor, etc.

7. *Make your wishes known* – This piece of advice is obviously not limited to financial issues, but it is vitally important to make your wishes known when transferring financial holdings or any other assets with significant value like; antiques, valuable collections, etc. before your transition. Also, it is important to make your wishes known regarding your funeral and burial arrangements, believe me it will keep down less confusing. This is especially true today since there are many "blended families" made up of children united by remarriage of the parents.

The bottom line is to write it all down in an organized matter and put the letter or notes where they can be found. While in law school, I had a law professor to tell us, "A short pencil is better than a long memory." Once again, make sure you consult with an attorney regarding these legal matters and the preparation of the legal documents.

This chapter is not meant to be entertaining or depressing to read, but a subject filled with information that can be helpful in a time of need. The following story was told about a woman who wanted her dead son brought back to life:

Once there was a woman named Kisagotami, whose first-born son died. She was so stricken with grief that she roamed the streets carrying the dead body and asking for help to bring her son back to life. A kind and wise man took her to the Buddha. The Buddha told her, "Fetch me a handful of mustard seeds and I will bring your child back to life." Joyfully Kisagotami started off to get them. Then the Buddha added, "But the seeds must come from a family that has not known death." Kisagotami went from door to door in the whole village asking for the mustard seeds, but everyone said, "Oh, there have been many deaths here," "I lost my father," "I lost my sister." She could not find a single household that had not been visited by death. Finally, Kisagotami returned to the Buddha and said, "There is death in every family. Everyone dies. Now I understand your teaching." The Buddha said, "No one can escape death and unhappiness. If people expect only happiness in life, they will be disappointed."

The obvious moral to the above story is that everyone, inescapable, has or will experience death/transition of a love one during his or her life experience while existing on this earthly plane. The death/transition of a loved one can be a devastating loss. My humble suggestion is to do whatever you can within your human power to lessen the grief and unhappiness you may experience doing the transition of a loved one. Everyone grieves differently so there is no prescribed methodology for how one should grieve. Here are some suggestions to help lessen the impact both emotionally and mentally:

1. Know that you are entitled to all of your feelings and emotions. During the first year you will probably feel numb. You may experience intense anger, guilt, denial and fear, all of which are normal for a bereaved person. After the first anniversary of your loved one's death/ transition, the numbness begins to wear off and the true reality hits you very hard. Many people say that the second year is the hardest. I believe our brain creates this numbness to protect us from going insane to keep from feeling the full blunt of the loss all at once; plus during that first year, the support from other family members and friends is very good.

2. Know that there is no timetable on your grieving process. Every individual is just that, an individual unique unto him or herself. There are many similarities in the pro-

cesses a bereaved person goes through, however, each person's journey is different depending on the diversity of our life's experiences. Know that it is scientifically proven that a loss of this magnitude is similar to a major physical injury.

3. Be very gentle and understanding to yourself. Grief must be selfish in order to survive, put yourself first, remember if you do not take care of yourself, you will not be much good to your surviving loved ones and friends. Know that you are not going insane and you are not crazy that you are just like any other person experiencing the loss of a loved one. If you can, take time off from work, although a quick return to work could be good therapy to divert your thoughts from your loss. Sleeping and eating every day is very important, do not indulge in alcohol and illegal drug use, as these are downers and will increase your state of depression severely. Do not let anyone dictate to you how you should or should not grieve, only you know deep inside what is the best for you; but know it is alright to take time off from grieving, so you may smile, laugh and enjoy your life.

4. Set healthy boundaries for yourself by giving yourself space and time to grieve. Know that it is okay to isolate yourself and grieve in private, however balance is very important in all aspects of the grief journey. Find a support group or network of individuals that understand your loss, such as local meetings for grief support, your religion institution and read books about grief.

5. It can be very healthy to create a memorial for the lost of your loved one; this can be in your home or garden.

6. Wait at least one year before making any major decisions such as, relocating, divorce, large purchases, etc.

7. Receiving counseling may help. A good grief therapist or counselor can be difficult to find, however it is worth seeking one out for assistance. Be sure to interview the counselor over the phone before scheduling an appoint- ment, ask questions like: have you counseled bereaved client before; have you study Thanatology (the study of death) and are you capable of providing grief counsel- ing; ask if they counsel from a religion perspective; ask what is their methodology in treating depression and post traumatic stress disorder. By asking the above ques- tions, you will know if this is the right counselor for you and your situation.

8. Prescription medication may help, however it will not dissolve your pain. Many grieving persons find that medication for sleep is a necessity; also medication for anti-anxiety or anti-depression helps them to cope bet- ter. Know that there are many variations of these medi- cations and finding the right one that works best is of- ten a daunting task, but may be worth it providing if it helps in the long run. Try not to sweat the small stuff, be strong and survive, know that you are not alone, just reach out for help, it is out there.

I understand that this chapter has been less than cheerful, but as I previously stated above in this chapter, it is meant to be informational and helpful when needed. I know the impact of the death/transition of a loved one is so profound that it reaches to the very core of our being and effects every aspect of our life physically, emotionally, mentally, socially and spiritually. However, we must all face the inevitability of life none of us are guaranteed to see tomorrow, so pre-death/transition planning is an intelligent and common sense thing to do; especially for anyone who wants to make it easier for their survivors. Do not be liked the man described in the Chinese Proverb that says, "A foolish man wait to dig a well when he is dying of thirst." We must know and except that there will come a time for our spirits to stand naked and be accountable to the universe. So put your emotions aside and proceed with your pre-death/transition planning, it will save your love ones from a lot of misery and uncomfortable moments.

Here are my *Wardisms* on the subject, "Death/Transition:"

Do not be a slave remain brave all the way
to your grave knowing you been saved.

W

Do not let your dreams melt like ice cream.

W

You have, unequivocally, satisfied your
life's test by achieving your very best.
So now is the time for you to take your
eternal rest.

W

Many years filled with tears may come and go, but
keep your flow as you grow and maintain life's glow.

W

As babies we enter the world with our fists
closed ready to grab on to life. When we
die our hands are opened, because we have
given all to life.

W

This world inhabits people who enter to
fulfill their individual missions and/or
place, then they make their transition to
another place in time and space.

W

Oh what a wonderful joy knowing a fetus
exist in a mother's womb. Oh what sad emotions
love ones display when the body
is placed to rest in a tomb.

W

During your life did you think it through and did not
sink or blink when it got rough, because in the end it
is all written in ink?

W

Now that my life is complete I can say, "I
walked and talked with all people even
kings and queens and all those in between."

W

I can unequivocally say there are:
No more clothes to wear
No more noise to hear
No more fears
No more years
It is all done, now I come to rest at
my eternal home.

W

You cannot delay, shave or wave your way
to your grave – just be brave and know
you have paved your way by living a good
righteous life day by day along the way.

**NATURE HAS AWAY OF CORRECTING
ITSELF**

THIS IS THE WAY NATURE PLANNED IT

Afterword

These four topics I chose to write about, *Self, Life, Relationship* and *Death* are the governing means by which humankind exists. This conclusion is not a delusion or even an illusion; I am just trying to provide you with a philosophy, a guide, a blueprint and/or a road map to live by; they are messages for a lifetime. When we know who we are, what we are, why we are and where we are as we travel this life journey, then we truly know, *Self.* When we truly know ourselves it becomes easier to be at peace, to be happy, to be kind and to be lovingly toward others. Then you are able to live a meaningful productive *Life,* serve humanity and build a better world for generations to come. When our life experiences are meaningful to us, we then devote a great deal of time to helping others and without question our *Relationship/Welationship* with our mates take on a new and different loving solidify meaning in every aspect. At some point time, having satisfied the three above areas of living, we make our transition into another place in time and space, commonly called *Death* to rest peacefully.

I have not written anything with the intent to anger or cause you to reject your teachings or personal beliefs, but quite the contrary. I am only asking you to stop retreating to your little personal cocoon (safe environment), but to step out into the world, embrace it and enjoy all its beautiful magnificence. I felt extremely compelled with a moral imperative to write this book in order to:

1. Inspire you to know who you are and embrace your divine greatness. Also, to conduct your own in-depth research and investigation into areas of concerned.

2. Motivate you to express being the best you can be and contribute to the betterment of the world (we all have something to offer).

3. Provoke you to think outside the norm from the way you have been accustomed to think. It is my fervent hope, wish and prayer that you will broaden your horizon and not be afraid to explore uncharted territories, which this vast universe has to offer.

4. Amuse you with my *Wardisms*, but yet fostering profundity to instigate deep thought.

We have made life so complex that we have lost sight as to why we are here, which is too be the keepers and protectors of humanity. Also, through our life experiences we must learn to act and live out the qualities of humanity, which are:

- Being humane to each other
- Being benevolent to each other
- Being kind to each other
- Being merciful to each other

What a glorious world this will be when we really understand, know and accept the laws that the Almighty Divine Supreme Creator has set forth for us to live by. We must accept the fact that the universe judges us on the good we contribute to humanity and not the bad seeds we sow to destroy it. I have written this book to open the minds, eyes and ears of those in need of a challenge and a different way to view and live their life experiences. The information contained in this book affords each of you the opportunity to stop philosophizing about the majors and minors of life, as well as seeing your life experiences from wrong side out, up side down and/or backwards. Further, it is up to each of you to add to the greatness of humanity by writing your own chapter or even your own book. Remember, as I have previously stated throughout my writings, "There is no truth until you decide your own truth." So trust in your heart and believe in what will work best for you. Remember, your body and mind know what is right and wrong for it. Our bodies and minds speak to us all the time, we must learn to listen to them. In David R. Hawkins, M.D., Ph.D., book titled, *Power Vs Force The Hidden Determinants of Human Behavior* stated, "Consciousness automatically chooses what it deems best from moment to moment because that ultimately is the only function of which it is capable." For these reasons you must be willing to transform your life experience by making a paradigm shift in the way you think. Furthermore, you must stop accepting erroneous premises hoping your conclusions will be right. It is imperative that you know and accept that you have an awesome responsibility to right the wrongs of those things, which are within your control and power. This will make the world a better place in which to live for generations to come. We must do whatever is right to build a better world and stop sitting around dreaming. The world is full of dreamers who never stop dreaming. To achieve our dreams we must do whatever righteously it will take to bring them into fruition, as oppose to sitting around wishing, moping and hoping our dreams will manifest themselves.

It is my fervent hope, wish and prayer that through my books I have provided my readers with a full plate of mind food to nurture their conscious. I hope you will use this mind food to think outside of the box by incorporating this transforming paradigm into your life experiences. Further, I hope these life messages I put forth in this book will undo and heal some of the pain, failure, suffering and misunderstanding you might be going through in your life experiences. I feel this will help you become a more joyful kinder person toward humankind and yourself. In addition, I hope this information will recontextulize and elevate your thinking to a level where you are able to integrate your mind and spirit, in order to express your innate Divinity, which you rightfully inherited at birth. I trust that my love will shine forth though my writings to help my readers experience their own inner peace, love, joy, and well-being. My food for thought is meant to be enlightened, inspirational, motivational, provocative and entertaining. Also, my intent is to inspire and help everyone, who is open and receptive, rise to a level of having peace, love and joy in their life experiences, which is the supreme essence of humankind existence. I deeply trust that I have achieved this awesome undertaking. I beseech you to find peace within yourself, humankind and this world you inhabit by meeting force with gentleness and impatience with patience. Henceforth, you have no logical reason to continue living your life experiences in the darkness of your thoughts. I trust my writings will be received admirably.

Know and accept that nothing trumps truth and wisdom.

BE YE DIVINE ULTIMATELY TRANSFORMED BY THE RENEWING OF YOUR THOUGHTS!

THE BEGINNING

Bibliography

The Living Bible, Wheaton, IL, Tyndale House Publishers, 1971.

The Encyclopedia of Marriage and The Family, volume 2.

The American Heritage Dictionary of the English Language, 4th ed. Boston: Houghton Miffin, 2006.

The Oxford Dictionary Of World Religions. Edited by Bowker: Oxford, New York: Oxford University Press, 1997.

Ashby, Muata A. *Mystical Wisdom Teachings And Meditations. Miami, FL:* Cruzian Mystic Books, 1996.

Beckwith, Michael A. *40 Day Mind Fast Soul Feast.* Calif.: Devores & Company, 2000.

Buettner, Dan. *The Blue Zone.* Washington, D.C.: National Geographic, 2008.

Corrigan, John, Frederick M. Denny, Carlos M. N. Eire, and Martin S. Jaffee. *Reading in Judaism, Christanity, and Islam.* Upper Saddle River, New Jersey: Prentice Hall, 1998.

Dyer, Wayne W. *The Power of Intention.* Carlsbad, Calif.: Hay House, 2004.

Gaer, Joseph. *The Wisdom of the Living Religion.* New York: Dodd, Mead & Company, 1956.

Hawkins, David R., M.D., Ph.D., *Power VS. Force The Hidden Determinants of Human Behavior.* California: Hay House, Inc., 2002.

Heinlein, Robert. *Time Enough for Love.* New York: The Berkeley Publishing Group, 1973.

Hendricks, Jr., Obery M., *The Politics of Jesus.* New York: Three Leaves Press, 2006.

Levy, Susan L., D.C. and Carol Lehr, M.A., *Your Body Can Talk.* Prescott, AZ : HOLM Press, 1996.

Mandino, Og. *The Greatest Miracle In The World.* New York: Bantam Books, Inc., 1975.

Martin, Tony. *Message To The People.* Dover, Mass.: The Majority Press, 1986.

Morris, Mary. *Young Lions.* Melrose Park, IL: MDM Publishing, 2009.

Moses, Jeffrey. *Oneness Great Principles Shared By All Religions.* New York: Ballantine Books, 2002.

Pearson, Carlton. *The Gospel of Inclusion.* New York: Atria Books, 2006.

Russell, Walter. *The Message Of The Divine Iliad.* Virginia: University of Science and Philosophy, 1971.

Russell, Lao. *God Will Work With You But Not For You.* Virginia: University of Science and philosophy, 1981.

Sacred Books of China: The Texts of Taoism. Trans. James Legge, D.D., L.L.D. London: Oxford University Press, 1891.

Sacred Books of the East (including the Vedic Hymns and the Dhammapada of Buddhism). Rev. ed. New York: P. F. Collier & Sons, 1900.

Sacred Books of the East: Laws of Manu. Trans. George Buhler. Oxford: Clarendon Press, 1886.

Sacred Books of the East. The Upanishads. Trans. F. Max Muller. Oxford: Clarendon Press, 1879.

Tomlin, Graham. *The Seven Deadly Sins And How To Overcome Them.* Oxford: Lion Book, 2007.

Ward, Isiah Paul, J.D. *Universal Cosmic Messages For Courtship And Marriage.* Willowbrook: Millennium Bridge, Inc., 2004.

Ward, Isiah Paul, J.D. *Wardisms For Self Development And Relationship Building.* Willowbrook: Millennium Bridge, Inc., 2006.

Ward, Isiah Paul, J.D. *Wardisms Naked Truth For Successful Living.* Willowbrook: Millennium Bridge, Inc., 2007.

Internet Sources:

See Wikipedia, *Healing Through Fasting,* http://en.wikipedia/wiki/

See Wikipedia, *Mental Health Disorder,* http://en.wikipedia/wiki/

See Wikipedia, *Emotional Freedom Technique,* http://en.wikipedia/wiki/

See Wikipedia, *Seven Deadly Sins,* http://en. wikipedia/wiki

See Wikipedia, *Tai chi chuan,* http://en.wikipedia/wiki/

See Wikipedia, *The System for Self Healing,* http://en.wikipedia/wiki/

About The Author

Isiah Paul "The Prophet" Ward, J.D. is a native of Atlanta, Georgia. He is the son of the late Rev. and Mrs. Isiah Paul Ward, Sr. He has lived in the Chicago, Illinois area for the last thirty-one years. He received a Bachelor of Science Degree in criminal justice from Georgia State University and a Juris Doctor from John Marshall School of Law. He has served as a mediator for the Circuit Court of Cook County, Illinois in various court cases. He has counseled numerous couples and singles on marital and relationship issues and is affectionately called the " relationship guru" along with known as "The Prophet." He is a member of numerous social, civic and educational organizations. Isiah is a powerful orator with a mission to educate those who are seeking knowledge. He is the author of the following books:

- *Universal Cosmic Messages for Courtship and Marriage*
- *Wardisms for Self Development and Relationship Building*
- *Wardisms Naked Truth for Successful Living*